THE PENNSYLVANIA CORRUPTION MACHINE

RUNNING IN FULL CAPACITY TO NEUTRALIZE THE TRUTH

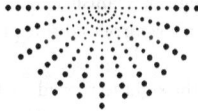

BEN WOOD JOHNSON

Edited by
WOLDEN OLIVIER

TESKO

Tesko Publishing
General Editor: Wolden Olivier

ISBN-13: 978-1-948600-97-2
ISBN-10: 1-948600-97-8

The first edition was printed in 2025 (printed in the United States)

Translated and edited by Ben Wood Johnson

Format: Pocket Book (Paperback)

www.teskopublishing.com

If you want to know more about Tesko Publishing, contact BWEC LLC/My Eduka Solutions at: 330 W. Main St # 214, Middletown, PA 17057, USA

To my children

CONTENTS

PREFACE

I am Dr. Benjamin Wood Johnson. As the author of the book you hold in your hand, I became Ms. Oliver's only advocate in a sea of deceitful actors. They fought tooth and nail to take me down. They attacked me personally, professionally, mentally, psychologically, and spiritually (through black magic, spells, and other occult means). It has been a tough journey for me; it has also been a tough journey for my children, particularly my young son, Wolden, who had been systematically targeted and ultimately became the latest casualty of intimidation when he was detained at the Fort Jackson Army base in July 2025 under false pretenses for several days.

What happened in this case? It is a critical question that underscores the failures at multiple levels, from the individual to institutional and systemic failures. The repercussions of these actions extend far beyond just one student, which highlights a pervasive issue within the educational and legal systems.

I hope that you are not the type to view skepticism toward government officials as being conspiratorial in nature. In fact, the government seldom tells the truth. If [and when] they do tell the truth, it is likely because the verity suits a particular narrative or it fits a particular political objective. At this juncture, the goal in compiling this book is not necessarily to convince you that the Commonwealth of Pennsylvania is evil. The aim is to let you come up with your own assessment of the state's conduct in this instance.

As the author of this title, I want to share the truth about this case as candidly as possible. While this book is not biographical in the accurate sense of the term, it is a true story, of which I am a part. Put differently, this book is not fictional. Rather, it is based on real people, real incidents, actual decisions, and real consequences, at least for Ms. Oliver and her family. Therefore, the story I narrate in the present context is real to the extent of my own experience. It is also a reflection of my knowledge and understanding of what transpired between 2023 and 2025.

Despite the above confessions, the book is neither a biography nor is it a speculative piece of literature. It does not imagine the realities of the individuals mentioned here. Rather, the discussion presented throughout these pages is based on the ongoing nature of the situation. However, there is no way to state, at least conclusively, how the story ended or will end.

At this point, I can only wish you an enjoyable reading experience. Please do share this book with your friends and family if you find it interesting enough for your own edification about the intersection between racism, at the most benign level, to systemic discrimination, at the pinnacle of the American government. Remember, racism is more poignant when it is masked by a veneer of legitimacy. Racism is more potent when the oppressors are the ones with Black faces and an unmistakable hue of African descent.

Thank you for picking up the present edition, which depicts the ongoing saga of the Oliver-Johnson family. Please, enjoy this reading. Let it inform you; let it show you a side of America, particularly the Pennsylvania Government, which you probably did not know existed in the history of race relations in that part of the world.

— Benjamin Wood Johnson
Elizabethtown, Pennsylvania (August 2025)

PROLOGUE (BY WOLDEN OLIVIER)

Germine Oliver's story is not just a personal tragedy; it is a case study in the systemic failures that plague higher education and the legal system. There, powerful institutions, like Pennsylvania State University, are shielded from accountability. Students who dare challenging discrimination[1] and retaliation[2] are left to navigate a labyrinth of procedural violations and institutional bias.

As a doctoral student[3] at Penn State's Ross and Carol Nese College of Nursing, Ms. Oliver faced a cascade of injustices that began with a discriminatory act, which led to a series of fraudulent actions and misconduct from university officials.

This experience culminated in her unlawful dismissal on January 31, 2024, by the very individual that she named in her complaint. Ms. Oliver's fight to hold the university accountable revealed a deeply entrenched system, which is dubbed here as the

---

1. Addressing discrimination requires awareness, education, and proactive measures to promote inclusion, equality, and social justice.
2. Retaliation refers to the act of returning an injury or wrong done to someone, often as a means of revenge or punishment.
3. A doctoral student is an individual who is pursuing a doctoral degree, such as a Ph.D. or a doctorate in a specific field of study.

"Pennsylvania Corruption Machine." This lethal machinery is designed to protect the powerful at the expense of the vulnerable, particularly minority and immigrant students who lack the resources and connections to fight back.

The first layer of systemic failure in Ms. Oliver's case lies in higher education itself, where universities like Penn State often prioritize their reputation and institutional interests over fairness and equity for students. Other institutions and state agencies banded together with the university to smear and to defame Ms. Oliver and her family. They sought to create a chilling effect on the family's resolve to hold them accountable and to admonish any efforts on their part to seek justice. This is emblematic of a culture that undermines the very principles of education and support that students should expect.

In this case, the *Pennsylvania corruption machine* was running at full capacity to neutralize Ms. Oliver and her family. A broad array of state agencies got involved in the matter with the sole purpose of neutralizing the threat, which they saw in Ms. Oliver and her family. Remarkably, her husband, Dr. Johnson, became public enemy number one in the corruption machine's quest to silence the family. They subsequently attacked their son, Wolden, using the US Army in a devious plan to unalive the young man as punishment for the family's daring ploy to assert their rights in Pennsylvania.

It is worth noting that this book is still a work in progress. While the Pennsylvania Human Relations Commission (also known as the PHRC)[4] initially dismissed and ultimately closed the case on November 6, 2024, they reopened the case on February 19, 2025, while the matter was still on appeal for review. However, they reopened the case after issuing legal

---

4. The Pennsylvania Human Relations Commission (PHRC) is a state agency that focuses on promoting equal opportunity and eliminating discrimination through enforcement of civil rights laws in Pennsylvania.

threats to the family, notably Dr. Johnson in no uncertain terms. The agency backtracked after Ms. Oliver, assisted by her husband, Dr. Johnson, raised concerns about fairness. The family pointed out numerous irregularities in the final decision by this civil rights agency to dismiss the case, including the agency's Executive Director (Chad Dion Lassiter) who had a conflict of interest in the matter, as he was honored by the university in a public banquet during the investigation period and failed to recuse himself.

> The PHRC is responsible for investigating complaints of discrimination based on various factors such as race, sex, age, religion, and disability in areas including employment, housing, and public accommodations. The PHRC works to educate the public about civil rights issues, facilitate dispute resolution, and ensure compliance with anti-discrimination laws to foster a fair and inclusive society.

Despite the PHRC's reversal, the matter is still in limbo. As of July 2025, the case is still unresolved, given the final decision is contested. On July 25, 2025, in a coordinated attack against the family, the PHRC recycled their November 6, 2024, decision and closed the case without any further explanations. The July decision was entered concurrently as the family's son was detained at Fort Jackson, South Carolina, a place where the Retired Army Colonel from Penn State, a person at the center of the discrimination complaint. During the son's repeated torture at the infamous military base, he was repeatedly reminded that his parents dared to challenge Penn State; he shall pay the price for that insolence, one drill sergeant hinted while battering the young man senselessly at Fort Jackson.

Everything mentioned thus far may seem improbable or even impossible. Yet, they are truthful accounts of what transpired between 2023 and 2025; these conducts are ongoing. They are backed by substantiated evidence, including emails, texts, audios, and video conversations.

As of August 16, 2025, the family appealed the July 25 copy-paste decision and raised substantial administrative and procedural defects for an immediate vacatur. However, the PHRC has not contacted Ms. Oliver; it has instead created numerous obstacles for the family. The agency has refused to investigate other complaints from family members. The PHRC has encouraged the family to go to the Court of Common Pleas instead, as this route is [seemingly] perceived as potentially more beneficial to Penn State and the PHRC in the long run. At the same time, no one in Pennsylvania would represent the family in any legal proceeding. There is no tangible alternative path for redress in this case. Justice is not only denied but also used as a mechanism to continue harming the family.

The case is unresolved at other state agency levels, including the PDE. Also, federal authorities, notably at the DOJ, OCR, and SPPO, have not responded to various complaints, leading family members to believe that state and federal officials are acting in concert with local authorities to silence them at all costs. As of August 2025, several complaints are pending or are unresolved. The state agencies in question have not reached or communicated a final decision about their investigation.

The case has reached a criminal degree, as investigations are tainted by a series of misstatements, inaccuracies, and lies, which had been entered and/or made to state officials during the official investigation. The family believes that these false statements must be ascertained and resolved under laws related to unworn statements to public authorities before any decision can be made about this case. Given the events outlined in the present context, Ms. Oliver's case is a developing story where harm to the family is ongoing, though also condoned by government officials. Thus, the conclusions echoed in these pages are based solely on a hypothetical rendering of how the case could end or could have been resolved in a court of law.

Germine Oliver's case depicts an interesting, but also a demoralizing, story about student rights, discrimination, and state involvement in misconduct. This case, as will be apparent later, is not limited to academia, as it does not relate solely academic issues. This is a modern-day conspiracy, which is reminiscent of the old days of the mafia in Philadelphia. The entities involved in this matter have revealed the true nature of their power and influence when it comes to minority students and their families.

This is a book about race, class, gender, ethnicity, and country of origin. Many of the individuals involved in the case share a commonality: they are Caucasian. Others belong to a specific social category. They saw, and ostensibly, treated the Oliver-Johnson family as if they are less-than, what ever that *reductibility* means to them and within their own context. It was as if the family does not deserve the rights guarantee to every citizen in this country. When the family insisted in asserting their rights, agency's reflex consisted of blatantly ignoring them in the most abject manner. The disdain was palpable, thus irrefutable as well, and it was by design.

Every effort had been deployed to undermine the case, the complainant, and her family. The intrigue and the linguistic maneuvers used to defeat a legitimate discrimination complaint was staggering. Did they succeed? I will let you be the judge of that, as you thumb through the next few chapters.

— *Wolden Olivier*
Elizabethtown, Pennsylvania (August 2025)

1
UNDERSTANDING THE CONCEPT OF DISCRIMINATION

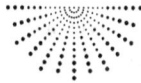

Discrimination is not a novel phenomenon in education. This reality is particularly pervasive in higher education. The concept refers to the unjust or prejudicial treatment of individuals or groups based on characteristics such as race, gender, age, sexual orientation, religion, disability, or other attributes. It manifests in various forms, including social, economic, and legal inequalities, and can occur at both individual and systemic levels.

Discrimination can lead to significant negative impacts on the targeted individuals or groups. It can limit their opportunities. It can marginalize the victim's voices and experiences. Discrimination can perpetuate cycles of disadvantage and inequality within society.

An important aspect of discriminatory conduct is retaliation. As the appellation implies, retaliation is the act of retaliating against one person or groups of individuals based on race, gender, or other protected characteristics. Retaliation itself, though a separate conduct, often succeed a discriminatory conduct. Therefore, retaliation is a part of discrimination.

Retaliation can manifest in various forms, including physical, emotional, or verbal actions taken in response to perceived harm, and is commonly observed in personal relationships, workplace dynamics, and international conflicts. Retaliatory behaviors may be driven by a desire for justice, retribution, or the restoration of one's reputation, but they can also escalate conflicts and lead to a cycle of ongoing aggression. In many contexts, such as employment law, retaliation is considered unlawful if it arises as a response to protected activities, like reporting discrimination or harassment, notably in the context of an educational setting.

The present situation involves a doctoral student enrolled at a prestigious state institution. Doctoral students often aim to develop expertise in their area of focus, culminating in the completion of a dissertation or thesis that demonstrates their findings and analytical skills. This advanced level of education typically involves conducting original research, engaging in rigorous academic coursework, and working closely with faculty advisors to contribute new knowledge to their discipline. The journey can be demanding, requiring dedication, critical thinking, and a commitment to scholarly inquiry.

In the example that follows here, a doctoral student experienced discrimination, as she felt her treatment was different from other students in the program. When she reported the individuals involved in the conduct she experienced, the university retaliated and punished her. The student was ultimately dismissed from the program and removed from the university despite completing all course requirements for degree completion. The student was left without any recourse and remedy, as both university and state officials stood against the student.

THE GENESIS OF THE ABUSE

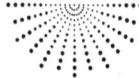

S ince 2023, the Pennsylvania State University,[1] particularly the Penn State's Ross and Carol Nese College of Nursing,[2] engaged in a targeted campaign against a Black, female, immigrant, and a student over the age of forty.[i] These characteristics place Ms. Oliver as a protected class individual within the American's current legal framework and judicial system for issues related to civil rights, notably retaliation and discrimination. Ms. Oliver was targeted academically. She was also beleaguered professionally and personally, a situation that toll a toll on her personal well-being.

University attacks later intensified and extended to Ms. Oliver's entire family, conspicuously her husband and their three children. University officials orchestrated a series of actions to

---

1. Pennsylvania State University, commonly known as Penn State, is a major public research university located in University Park, Pennsylvania. Established in 1855, it is one of the largest universities in the United States, offering a wide range of undergraduate and graduate programs across various fields of study.
2. Penn State's Ross and Carol Nese College of Nursing is a prominent nursing education institution within Pennsylvania State University that focuses on preparing highly skilled and compassionate nursing professionals.

discredit the family, which included lies, mischaracterizations of the situation, and flat-out fraud. The goal was to undermine the family at all costs.

The university, via its trusted political allies, activated the "Pennsylvania corruption machine" to go after the very people that it victimized. This statement is not an exaggeration. Rather, this rendering of the situation is an accurate description of how multiple institutions, particularly the Pennsylvania Disciplinary Board,[3] Pennsylvania State University, the Pennsylvania Human Relations Commission (PHRC), the local police department, and even federal liaisons like the OCR (Office of Civil Rights)[4] and SPPO (Student Privacy Policy Office)[5] enlisted themselves to defeat the family by engaging in the following activities:[ii]

1. Coordinating responses
2. Suppressing evidence
3. Retaliating against protected activity
4. Deliberately avoiding accountability

The family faced not just a rogue university but has also been confronted by a closed system of institutional actors who are protecting each other. They did so not because the facts are unclear, but because the truth would expose them all. The signs of systemic corruption are irrefutable in this case. They include:

1. Cover-up instead of investigation.

---

3. The Pennsylvania Disciplinary Board is an authority established to oversee the professional conduct of attorneys in the state of Pennsylvania.
4. The OCR, or the Office of Civil Rights, is a division within various governmental agencies, primarily the U.S. Department of Education and the U.S. Department of Health and Human Services, tasked with enforcing civil rights laws and ensuring compliance with nondiscrimination policies.
5. The Student Privacy Policy Office (SPPO) is an entity focused on safeguarding the privacy of student information in educational institutions.

2. Fabricated procedural hurdles (e.g., POA/Power of Attorney demands).[6]
3. Delay tactics with no lawful basis.
4. Retaliation against lawful complaint activity.
5. Coordination between state and federal actors to shut down any complaint related to the case.
6. Unwillingness to issue rulings, because any ruling might backfire.

This case illustrates a corruption machine in action. It epitomizes a series of bad-faith actors, who form a network of personal and political interests. Together, they grind forward to crush anything that threatens the network's survival, relevance, and continuity. This case exposes something that they never expected anyone to piece together: that is, the family's resilience and fortitude. As a result, they are now reacting like a machine with no off switch, only defensive programming.

Their conduct amounts to nothing short of a well-oiled machine designed to perform a specific task. In this case, the task of the corruption machine is to protect itself from public exposure. Ms. Oliver's case threatened the very existential nature of the Pennsylvania Corruption machine. They were in a full defensive mode.

The term "Pennsylvania Corruption Machine" typically refers to a perception or reality of systemic corruption within the political and governmental institutions of Pennsylvania. It suggests an entrenched network of unethical practices involving bribery, nepotism, kickbacks, and other forms of misconduct that compromise the integrity of public service. This phrase may also highlight specific scandals or the influence of powerful political

---

6. POA, or Power of Attorney, refers to a legal document that grants one individual (the agent or attorney-in-fact) the authority to act on behalf of another individual (the principal) in legal or financial matters.

figures and organizations that manipulate the political landscape for personal gain, often at the expense of the public interest. The term can evoke concerns about accountability, transparency, and the overall health of democratic processes in the state.

Moreover, it is worthy of note that a POA allows the appointed person to make decisions, sign documents, and manage affairs when the principal is unable to do so, whether due to illness, absence, or other circumstances. Demands related to a Power of Attorney may involve the execution of specific legal tasks, financial transactions, or healthcare decisions that the principal has empowered the agent to perform, and may also encompass the proper handling and presentation of the POA document in various situations.

---

i. Penn State is recognized for its strong emphasis on research, its vibrant campus life, and its athletic programs, particularly in football, which is a significant part of its identity. The university is also known for its commitment to community service and outreach, promoting engagement and leadership among its students.

Named in honor of benefactors Ross and Carol Nese, the college offers a comprehensive range of undergraduate and graduate nursing programs, emphasizing both clinical practice and research. It aims to address healthcare needs through innovative education, interprofessional collaboration, and community engagement, while also fostering a commitment to diversity, equity, and inclusion within the nursing profession. The college's faculty and resources support students in becoming leaders in nursing and improving health outcomes within diverse populations.

ii. The primary function of the Pennsylvania Disciplinary Board is to investigate complaints against lawyers regarding ethical violations or misconduct, including issues related to dishonesty, fraud, and other breaches of legal and professional standards. The board is part of the Pennsylvania Supreme Court's system for maintaining the integrity of the legal profession, ensuring that attorneys adhere to the rules of professional conduct, and protecting the public from misconduct by legal practitioners. It also provides a framework for discipline, which can range from reprimands to disbarment, depending on the severity of the infraction.

The OCR's main objectives include protecting individuals from discrimination based on race, color, national origin, sex, disability, and age in educational programs and activities, as well as healthcare services. The OCR investigates complaints, provides guidance on compliance, and promotes equal access to educational and health opportunities, striving to foster environments that uphold civil rights and support diversity and inclusion.

The SPPO develops, implements, and oversees policies and practices that ensure compliance with relevant privacy laws, such as the Family Educational Rights and Privacy Act (FERPA). The SPPO also provides guidance and resources for schools, educational agencies, and stakeholders to protect student data from unauthorized access and mishandling, fostering a secure learning environment while supporting transparency and accountability in the management of student information.

3
THE STORY

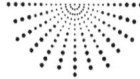

Since November 2022, Pennsylvania State University officials had their sights set on Germine Oliver, a female student from the Caribbean.[i] By that time, she had been a student in the DNP (Doctor of Nursing Practice)[ii] since 2018. She had taught a course in the program as a graduate student. University officials concocted a plan to remove her from the program, which came to fruition in early February 2023 and culminated in her formal dismissal on January 31, 2024.

By that time, Ms. Oliver had already completed all the required benchmarks for program or degree completion, excluding her final oral presentation. However, school officials were determined to find a way to dismiss Ms. Oliver. A week before her scheduled final oral presentation (November 2023),[1] the university canceled Ms. Oliver's final stage in the program and demanded that she redo the final project, a three-semester capstone, which is guided by a program chair.

While Ms. Oliver initially agreed to redo the project, she

---

1. This was the second cancelation of her oral presentation. The first cancelation occurred in February 2023.

reached out to other school officials, including the graduate school. The student raised concerns about the unfair treatment to which she had been subjected. This call led to a series of retaliatory actions, which also led to her receiving a failing grade on an independent course, which was supposed to be non-graded and designed for Ms. Oliver to complete her capstone requirements. The course, which the student herself requested and approved for the sole purpose of completing her project paper and making an oral presentation at the end of the semester, became the apparatus which, coincidentally as well, nursing school officials saw as a loophole to get rid of Ms. Oliver at all costs and by any means necessary.

THE ARMY COLONEL (KELLY WOLGAST)

The course instructor, a retired army colonel, known for being unabashedly tough and uncompromising, given her military background and her authoritative stance and unyielding academic style, changed the nature of the course toward the end of the semester. The retired colonel made several demands. But the more Ms. Oliver agreed to comply with her demands, the more the colonel increased them, which she conveyed as being nonnegotiable.

The colonel's interaction with Ms. Oliver became so adversarial that the power imbalance between the two was unequivocal. At some point, Ms. Oliver felt the need to ask the colonel to stop harassing her, a request that the colonel did not take lightly. Amid Ms. Oliver's repeated requests for the harassment to end, the colonel retaliated against the student in the most blatant manner.

The colonel failed Ms. Oliver in the independent study course despite her initial decision to give her a deferred grade on the course, which, by the way, was not supposed to be graded. The colonel acted with a level of confidence, which suggested that she was not acting alone. The unlawful grade, which came immediately after Ms. Oliver claimed that the colonel's demands amounted to harassment, was entered into the student's transcript and academic records. The grade came across as a punitive action designed to sabotage Ms. Oliver's academic future in retaliation for asserting her rights.

OFFICE OF EQUAL OPPORTUNITY AND ACCESS

On January 2, 2024, Ms. Oliver filed a discrimination complaint with the Pennsylvania State University Office of Equal Opportunity and Access (also known as OEOA). Ms. Oliver asserted that several faculty and administrators in the College of Nursing had discriminated against her and retaliated after she asserted her rights. The school initially acknowledged the complaint and offered to assist Ms. Oliver with mitigating the impact of the conduct she experienced. However, the OEOA was never sincere in its demarche.

They sought to contain the situation; they pretended to investigate the matter. Subsequently, they isolated Ms. Oliver; they tried to gaslight her.

Based on the advice from university officials and the institution's own Ombudsperson's recommendation, Ms. Oliver sought to register for the ongoing semester (Spring 2024). But the OEOA explicitly told Ms. Oliver not to contact other school officials while the investigation, which had not begun in earnest, was pending. That explicit demand also raised a few red flags, which led Ms. Oliver to ask about her academic status before engaging with investigators.

Ms. Oliver thought that knowing her academic status before the investigation started would determine what to expect from the investigation itself and the investigators. It was not clear that the OEOA was going to protect Ms. Oliver's rights or the university's interest. Ms. Oliver was unsure about the office's loyalty or obligation to investigate this matter impartially.

During the initial intake meeting on Zoom, Ms. Oliver planted the question to the university's representative, specifically via its OEOA Investigators. But they did not have an answer for her at the time. Yet, they tried to proceed anyway. Ms. Oliver insisted and persisted in asking for a clear response about her academic status.

Ms. Oliver informed the OEOA that she needed to know her current academic status at the university, as she is not registered for any course despite her attempts to do so. The student noted that she does not know how to engage with the OEOA without knowing her rights under university policies and the law. The investigators promised to inquire with the appropriate officials about Ms. Oliver's question. They agreed to postpone the initial intake questionnaire before proceeding further.

After the Zoom conversation, the OEOA went silent. They did not follow up on their initial promise to provide Ms. Oliver with the resources and the support that her situation required. Then, it became apparent that the office's initial interaction with Ms. Oliver was not a genuine response to addressing her situation. It also became clear that the whole thing was a subversive attempt to neutralize the complaint by pretending to investigate the claims, the outcome of which had already been determined by university officials.

It became painfully clear that the OEOA was not sincere, as they seemingly got caught off guard by Ms. Oliver's request to know her academic status. The office had lost control of the narrative when Ms. Oliver asked to know about her status within the university system before she committed herself to an investigation from the university's own investigative body, given the leadership status, the rank, and the administrative position held by the individuals named in the complaint and those who got involved in the matter post-complaint filling. It became undeniable that the OEOA's plan, perhaps that of the university to justify the retaliation against Ms. Oliver, backfired. The university's strategy fell apart.

A ROGUE ASSOCIATE DEAN (JUDITH HUPCEY)

As the situation became untenable for the university, they also became determined to get rid of Ms. Oliver. On January 24, 2024, Ms. Oliver reiterated her concerns about the university's violations of its own policies and formally requested a grade adjudication for her N596 independent study (Fall 2023). But the university ignored her call.

The administrator who was supposed to process Ms. Oliver's request for grade adjudication was not only the only person habilitated for such a process but was also named within Ms. Oliver's discrimination complaint. The administrator ignored Mr. Olier's repeated requests. But she did so callously.

The administrator ignored Ms. Oliver; she did so despite knowing (at least constructively) that other school officials were included in the communication. This action suggested that the university leadership had given the green light to go after Ms. Oliver; they did so despite knowing that Ms. Oliver could not be dismissed without concluding all academic matters.

On January 31, 2024, just 29 days after Ms. Oliver raised due process violations and other concerns about school policy violations, the same administrator who was not a member of Ms. Oliver's doctoral committee issued a dismissal letter. She stated that Ms. Oliver had failed the very course, which grade adjudication request she ignored. The administrator cited academic performance as the reason for the dismissal, which was inherently a unilateral decision based on vague and capricious rationales and demands. The failing grade from the independent study course, though not adjudicated, despite Ms. Oliver's many requests, was then used as a basis or as a pretext to dismiss her from the program.

POLICY VIOLATIONS TO JUSTIFY THE DISMISSAL

The dismissal and the subsequent actions by university officials violated Penn State's own policy (GCAC-803), which explicitly states that only a doctoral committee can determine the dismissal of a doctoral student for unsatisfactory scholarship, and that the process must culminate with a final decision by the Dean of the Fox Graduate School. The administrator's one-sided action bypassed both requirements for administrative oversight. She did so [ipso facto] and as hastily as possible to deny Ms. Oliver advance notice, an opportunity for review, and the procedural protections guaranteed by the policy. The goal was to force Ms. Oliver and her family to the Court of Common Pleas (the CCP)[2] where [presumably] they already had their designated judge waiting, a *corrupt person in a robe* who would then decide in the university's favor on procedural grounds, notwithstanding the merit of the case.

In a formal response to the PHRC, the university claimed that it dismissed Ms. Oliver for academic reasons and had "robust" policies in place. The university, via its attorneys and in a shocking move to discredit Ms. Oliver, lied about her explicit grade adjudication request, which was filed and sent to various university officials on January 24, 2024. While the school claimed

---

2. The Court of Common Pleas (CCP) is a trial court found in several U.S. states, mainly responsible for handling civil and criminal cases. Its jurisdiction typically includes a wide range of matters such as personal injury, contract disputes, property issues, and family law, depending on the specific state's laws. The CCP serves as the first level of appeal for certain lower court decisions and plays a crucial role in the judicial system by addressing cases that may not fall under the authority of specialized courts. The structure and functions of the CCP can vary by state, but it generally aims to ensure fair and equitable resolutions to legal disputes within its jurisdiction.

that the dismissal was based on academic reasons, the reality is Ms. Oliver was dismissed for a course that was supposed to be non-graded and non-adjudicated, as she completed all required courses in the program. Similarly, Ms. Oliver was not given the opportunity to be heard, as per school policies.

This violation was compounded by the glaring due process failure. The grade adjudication only occurred post-dismissal, after Ms. Oliver's reinstatement, which followed several letters of protest, which, in turn, confirmed that the grade was not final at the time of her dismissal, a clear violation of due process, as students are entitled to a fair opportunity to challenge academic decisions before adverse actions are taken. The administrator's conflict of interest, combined with the close temporal proximity between the discrimination complaint and the dismissal, demonstrated that the action was retaliatory, not academic, in nature. The university dismissed Ms. Oliver just days after her formal grade adjudication request without addressing the pending adjudication.

Not only did the university cite course failure as the basis for Ms. Oliver's dismissal, but the dean of the nursing school also made a fraudulent statement about Ms. Oliver's academic progress and her record. The dean cited a nonexistent course number to justify the dismissal. When Ms. Oliver challenged the false information about her academic records, the university remained silent. The school later refused to make corrections or even to allow Ms. Oliver to view her records under the Family Educational Rights and Privacy Act (FERPA).[3]

---

3. FERPA stands for the Family Educational Rights and Privacy Act. It is a United States federal law that was enacted in 1974 to protect the privacy of student education records. FERPA grants parents certain rights regarding their children's education records and provides students with the ability to access their own records once they reach the age of 18 or attend a postsecondary institution. Some key provisions of FERPA include: 1. The right to inspect and review the student's education records. 2. The right to request the amendment of records that are inac-

FILING COMPLAINTS AND THE COVER-UPS

Ms. Oliver filed several complaints with state and federal officials. However, these complaints were dismissed or referred to
the PHRC for adjudication. Ms. Oliver discovered that the
PHRC's Executive Director, Chad Dion Lassiter, had a public
engagement with the university days after signaling her intent to
reach out to the agency to the Dean of equity in a formal email.

On January 25, 2024, Ms. Oliver and her family filed a verbal
complaint against the university, one month before Lassiter's
involvement with the university on and around February 26,
2024. Mr. Lassiter gave a keynote address at the university
during a banquet. But he did not recuse himself from the case,
even as Ms. Oliver continued to reach out to the agency before,
during, and even after Lassiter's engagement with the institution
that his agency is investigating.

Despite the evidence presented, the PHRC, via its executive
director, Chad Dion Lassiter, later endorsed the university's
version of events, which includes making an additional false
statement about Ms. Oliver's academic record. The agency stated
that she had received two grades below a B as of May 2023,
which is demonstrably false, as per Ms. Oliver's transcript. When
Ms. Oliver and her family insisted on Mr. Lassiter's recusal from
the case, the agency targeted the family with legal threats and
engaged in retaliatory conduct, which included the agency's
refusal to investigate other complaints by family members and
the imposition of POA demands.

As will be apparent in the next few chapters as well,
Ms. Oliver faced enormous pushbacks from the university, via

---

curate or misleading. 3. The right to have some control over the disclosure of
personally identifiable information from the education records.

Under FERPA, schools must obtain written consent from parents or eligible
students before disclosing personally identifiable information, with certain
exceptions.

faculty and administrators. She experienced the same level of retaliation from government officials, which included both state and federal officials. A case in point is the involvement of the Pennsylvania Disciplinary Board, which is laid out in the book titled "Attorneys Can Lie in Pennsylvania.

In this case, the Pennsylvania Disciplinary Board went all the way. They revealed to anyone who might be curious to discover that they were not an impartial arbiter in this case. They have a horse in the game. The phrase "facing the Pennsylvania corruption machine" is not just valid in the present context. It is a testament of a truth, which, hopefully, will become irrefutable as you navigate this text and as you review the evidence presented at the end of the manuscript.

The disciplinary board of Pennsylvania made the point of referring to confidentiality to restrict any communication regarding its conduct. But I refused to be intimidated by corrupt public officials acting outside the realm of their duties and responsibilities. The law is clear and the violations are irrefutable. The board used evasive language to undermine the complaint, not o the merits, but on a desire to protect one of their own, given that one of the attorneys involved in the matter clerked for the court. See the book titled *Attorneys Can Lie in Pennsylvania* to learn more.

The board's confidentiality threats, though they may be grounded in sound administrative practices, were used, in my view, in this case, to intimidate the family. As the author of this compilation, I must reiterate it here as well, I take full responsibility for relating the issues as I have witnessed them and as I have experienced them. I have been involved in this case since the beginning. I initiated the first formal complaint against the university (August 2023).

I experienced discrimination and retaliation for advocating on Ms. Oliver's behalf. I have direct knowledge of the events. Therefore, I am within my rights to relate these issues as I know them to have occurred. I will not yield to the board's confidentiality threats, as they are designed to shield their conduct and that of the attorneys. However, the evidence is my only reference. I will not falter when it comes to brandishing the evidence as proof of misconduct in this case.

For the sake of argumentative cogency and literary brevity, it is worthy of note, the focus in the present context is not on the conduct displayed by the Pennsylvania Disciplinary Board. Their conduct epitomizes the notion of the Pennsylvania corruption machine in the most vivid manner. While the Board acted with little to no shame in expressing views that they knew, or had reasons to know, conflicted with the core of their mission to safeguard professional conduct in the legal profession, other actors played a significant role in greasing the wheels of this well-oil machine, which is described here [unequivocally and unapologetically] as the *Pennsylvania Corruption Machine*.

---

i. The Caribbean refers to a region consisting of the Caribbean Sea, its islands, and the surrounding coasts, characterized by diverse cultures, languages, and histories. The area includes more than 7,000 islands, islets, reefs, and cays, with notable islands such as Haiti, Jamaica, Barbados, and Puerto Rico. The Caribbean is known for its rich biodiversity, vibrant music and dance traditions, and a blend of influences from indigenous peoples, European colonizers, African slaves, and immigrant communities. Economically, the region relies heavily on tourism, agriculture, and fishing, while facing challenges such as climate change and economic vulnerability.

ii. DNP, or Doctor of Nursing Practice, is a terminal degree in the nursing profession that emphasizes advanced clinical practice, leadership, and evidence-based decision-making in healthcare settings. The DNP program is designed to prepare nurses to address complex healthcare challenges, improve patient outcomes, and influence healthcare policy. The DNP focuses on applying research findings to clinical practice, equipping graduates with the skills necessary to implement and evaluate health improvement initiatives and to work collaboratively across various healthcare systems.

4

FABRICATED SANCTIONS AND PROCEDURAL FRAUD

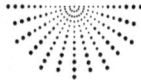

The Pennsylvania corruption machine's operation began with Pennsylvania State University, a public institution entrusted with shaping minds and upholding academic integrity. Instead, it targeted a Black immigrant mother, a dedicated scholar, and parent, with a vicious campaign of fabricated academic sanctions. The university accused her of violations that were never substantiated. They relied on vague allegations and shifting narratives.

To justify Ms. Oliver's dismissal, Penn State engaged in blatant procedural irregularities, which included manipulating evidence, ignoring its own policies, and retroactively altering regulations mid-case to create a veneer of legitimacy. For example, internal documents reveal that the university changed its academic misconduct policy after Ms. Oliver's case was initiated. They applied the new rules retroactively to ensure her expulsion and to protect the school official involved in the unlawful decision. This conduct was not an oversight. Rather, this was a calculated act of fraud, which was designed to eliminate Ms. Oliver's presence in the university and silence her contributions.

A CULTURE OF RETALIATION

As noted above, Ms. Oliver's dismissal was not an isolated incident. Instead, this was part of a broader pattern of retaliation against her family for their refusal to remain silent. As Ms. Oliver pursued appeals and filed complaints, Penn State escalated its retaliatory tactics. Faculty allies who supported Ms. Oliver or those who hinted at such intention were presumed pressured to withdraw their endorsements or the potential thereof.

In one instance, a former advisor was denied the opportunity to become a part of Ms. Oliver's doctoral committee as its chair. The goal was to prevent any uncontrolled influence on the desired outcome in the case. Other school officials who had initially claimed that Ms. Oliver's situation was unusual [and should not have happened] inexplicably changed their tune. That individual became part of the oppressive machine against Ms. Oliver.

A case in point to echo here is that of Sheldon Fields. As a faculty and diversity advocate, Fields was in the perfect position to help Ms. Oliver. He initially showed compassion for Ms. Oliver's ordeal. However, he later became one of the voices of the very oppressive machine that he had called out earlier against Ms. Oliver.

In the same way, Ms. Oliver's academic records were selectively altered. The goal was to cast doubt on her credentials or her academic capacity, as if to suggest that she was a mediocre student who deserved all the assaults the university did on her in the span of a few months. They did so notwithstanding that she had been enrolled in the program for over five years and had passed all the required benchmarks for degree completion.

NO LEGAL PROTECTION AGAINST ABUSE

The university's legal team at Buchanan Ingersoll & Rooney PC, a well-funded and deeply entrenched law firm, located across the United States, submitted demonstrably false information to external investigators. The law firm, via its attorneys, including, but not limited to, George C. Morrison, Esq. (PA 203223), Keith M. Lee, Esq. (PA 330237), and Andrew T. Simmons, Esq. (PA 331973), deliberately misrepresented academic timelines and fabricated events to demonize Ms. Oliver and to paint her as less than a deserving student. These lies were not minor errors; they were strategic.

These falsehoods, in my view, were intended to discredit the family's claims of mistreatment and to protect both the institution's reputation and the individuals involved in the situation, notably the retired Army Colonel (Kelly Wolgast) and the Associate Dean (Judith Hupcey), whose husband potentially had strong ties with prominent political figures, notably Josh Shapiro, the current governor of Pennsylvania, and the Dean of the Nursing School (Laurie Badzek), whose *ethnic background* seems to be the driving force behind the mafia-like response the Oliver-Johnson family experienced across multiple state and federal agencies.

The intent behind the university's actions was clear. They sought to maintain control of the narrative and silence dissent. They used all sorts of means to intimidate the family, including police visits, death threats, actual death in the family (homeland), legal threats, torture (U.S. Army), harassment, online doxing, entrapment, email fishing campaign, anonymous phone call threats, computer hacking and surveillance, AI manipulation, social media suppression and harassment, and unsolicited home visits by unknown individuals, among other intimidation strategies and tactics.

When confronted with documentary evidence, such as emails,

meeting minutes, and policy documents, that exposed their false-hoods, Penn State doubled down. They refused to correct Ms. Oliver's academic record or acknowledge wrongdoing, while admitting that they dismissed her and lied about the reason for their decision. This refusal to own up to their actions further showed the lengths to which the institution was willing to go to protect itself and its allies. The ongoing struggle described here illustrates the challenges faced by those who dared to challenge authority in such a powerful system.

Considering these troubling developments, it is evident that the issues at play extend far beyond the individual case of Ms. Oliver; they encapsulate a broader, systemic failure within the educational institution itself. They raise legitimate questions about the integrity of civil rights protections in academia. As institutions of learning hold the responsibility of fostering environments where students feel safe and valued, this case highlights a systemic abuse of power that not only harms individual students but undermines the fundamental principles of justice, equity, and accountability.

A SYSTEMIC PROBLEM

The willingness of the university's administration to manipulate facts and conceal the truth raises critical concerns regarding the adequacy of existing civil rights protections for students, particularly those who belong to marginalized communities. Without institutional accountability, there is little room for victims of abuse and mistreatment to seek redress effectively. This culture of silence and denial not only silences dissent but also perpetuates a hostile educational environment, where students may feel disenfranchised and powerless.

The intertwining of personal connections and political influence in this case underscores the urgent need to scrutinize the relationships between educational institutions and powerful individuals. The potential for conflicts of interest should compel policymakers and educational leaders to advocate for transparent practices and to establish independent review processes designed to strip away the insulating armor that allows institutions to evade accountability.

As we reflect on these events, it becomes crucial for stakeholders, students, parents, educators, and civil rights advocates to unite and demand robust protections that ensure equitable treatment for all students. They must do so irrespective of a student's background, be they academic or else, or personal circumstances. Reforming institutional policies to safeguard against retaliation, instituting training programs that focus on ethics and accountability, and creating avenues for independent oversight are essential steps toward creating a truly inclusive educational environment.

The struggle faced by Ms. Oliver and others who dare to challenge entrenched power systems highlights a critical moment in the fight for civil rights within education. Ensuring that every student can pursue an education free from abuse and retribution is not just a legal necessity but a moral imperative and a core component of a just society. Only through collective action and unwavering commitment can we hope to redefine the landscape of higher education as one where truth is celebrated, equity is prioritized, and every voice is heard.

As we reflect on the stories of resilience and determination exemplified by individuals like Ms. Oliver, it becomes painfully clear that the need for systemic change within educational institutions is urgent. The battles she has faced reveal not only the personal toll of standing against injustice but also the broader implications of ignoring the rights of vulnerable students. When educational settings fail to protect their members from discrimination and retaliation, they undermine the very purpose of learning: to foster a safe and inclusive environment where all can thrive. It is imperative that we continue to champion the value of accountability and empowerment within our institutions. We must ensure that all stakeholders, students, educators, and administrators alike, are committed to upholding civil rights in education.

Transitioning to the next critical angle of this discourse, we must delve into the role of oversight bodies in perpetuating or alleviating these challenges. In principles, oversights entities should hold state institutions accountable, as oversight bodies refer to organizations or entities established to monitor, regulate, and ensure accountability within specific sectors, institutions, or processes. They are supposed to oversee the actions of governments, corporations, or other organizations to ensure compliance with laws, standards, and ethical practices.

These bodies can take various forms, including regulatory agencies, independent commissions, or watchdog organizations, and their primary role is to promote transparency, prevent corruption, and protect public interests by conducting audits, evaluations, and investigations, as well as providing recommendations for improvement. The next section (Complicity of Oversight Bodies) will explore how these organizations, tasked with safeguarding student rights, can sometimes hinder progress rather than promote it. We can debate what reforms are essential to dismantle barriers that persist in our education systems.

5

THE COMPLICITY OF OVERSIGHT
BODIES

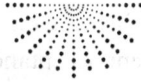

The issue of corruption within oversight bodies, particularly the Pennsylvania Human Relations Commission (PHRC) and the Office for Civil Rights (OCR), casts a long shadow over the landscape of civil rights in education. These institutions, which are ostensibly designed to protect the rights of students and ensure equitable access to education, often find themselves mired in bureaucratic inefficiencies and political ties that undermine their legitimacy and effectiveness. While families seek justice for discriminatory practices in schools, they are met instead with a convoluted maze of processes and a lack of genuine accountability.

This complicit atmosphere not only erodes public trust but also perpetuates a cycle of inequality that disproportionately affects marginalized communities. It is essential that these agencies rise above the entrenched corruption, acting with transparency and integrity to truly champion the rights of every student in Pennsylvania, so that the promise of an equal education can become a reality for all.

In exploring the troubling dynamics between the Pennsylvania Human Relations Commission (PHRC) and The Oliver-

Johnson family's pursuit of justice, it becomes evident that rather than serving its intended role as an advocate for civil rights, the PHRC's actions reflect a troubling betrayal of its mandate. The Oliver-Johnson family's experience illustrates a deeply flawed system where purported safeguards against discrimination are instead manipulated to protect powerful entities like Penn State.

The Commission's dismissal of a detailed complaint based on invented procedural requirements raises concerns about its commitment to truly investigating discrimination. This dismissal, and the subsequent acceptance of misleading information from the university against unmistakable evidence to the contrary, point to an alarming pattern of complicity. Such actions undermine the very foundation of the PHRC's purpose and instill a sense of distrust among those seeking justice.

As the family sought assistance from federal oversight bodies such as the Office for Civil Rights (OCR) and Ms. Oliver Privacy Policy Office (SPPO), their hopes for accountability were similarly dashed. These agencies, designed to uphold federal civil rights and privacy standards, not only failed to challenge the inadequacy of the PHRC but also employed evasive tactics to sidestep their responsibilities. This lack of support left the family feeling abandoned and without recourse as they tried to navigate an already challenging situation.

By mirroring the state's obstructionist approach and disregarding critical evidence, these federal entities effectively aligned themselves with the status quo. This alignment exacerbated the family's struggle for justice. This reality also left them feeling even more disillusioned with the system. The actions of these federal bodies contributed to a frustrating environment where progress toward an acceptable resolution seemed impossible.

The family found themselves navigating a bureaucratic labyrinth that served to entrench the very discrimination they were seeking to challenge. With each step they took, it appeared to lead to further hurdles, with no clear path to resolution. The compounded effect of this systemic failure deepened their sense of injustice and hopelessness.

THE PHRC'S BETRAYAL OF ITS MANDATE

In a just system, the Pennsylvania Human Relations Commission (PHRC), tasked with investigating discrimination and ensuring civil rights, would have been a beacon of hope for the family. Instead, it became a central cog in the corruption machine. When the family filed a detailed complaint outlining Penn State's discriminatory practices, the PHRC did not conduct a substantive investigation.

Rather, the agency deployed an arsenal of technicalities to dismiss the case without review. In an unprecedented move, the PHRC invented a requirement for a "Power of Attorney," a demand designed to block a valid third-party complaint filed on The Oliver-Johnson family's behalf. This requirement does not exist in its own regulations or state law, demonstrating a clear deviation from standard practices.

This was not a procedural quirk but a deliberate barrier, erected to shield the Pennsylvania State University from scrutiny. The actions of the PHRC reflected a troubling disregard for justice. They have left the family without the support and protection they sought. In a situation that should have fostered accountability, the commission's response exemplified the very issues of corruption and discrimination they were meant to combat.

The PHRC's complicity extended beyond inaction. It quietly accepted and repeated Penn State's false submissions, despite being presented with irrefutable evidence, such as time-stamped emails and official correspondence, that contradicted the university's claims. The reliance on misleading information shows a deep-seated disregard for the truth and the concerns of those who sought justice.

When the family pressed for accountability, the PHRC responded with delays, vague correspondence, and an outright refusal to engage with the merits of the case. This lack of transparency further emphasized the institution's unwillingness to confront the issues at hand. The family's desperation for resolution was met with a systematic avoidance of responsibility by the PHRC.

These tactics were not about upholding standards but about exhausting the family's resources and resolve. By dragging out the process and minimizing their concerns, the PHRC [effectively] ensured that the complaint would die in obscurity. The intent behind these strategies was not to fulfill their obligations but to stifle any meaningful pursuit of justice.

FEDERAL OVERSIGHT'S FAILURE: OCR AND SPPO

The Oliver-Johnson family's appeals to federal agencies, which include the Office for Civil Rights (OCR) and the Student Privacy Policy Office (SPPO), met a similar fate lie the way the PHRC conducted itself. These bodies, designed to oversee compliance with federal civil rights and privacy laws, should have intervened to correct the PHRC and Penn State's misconduct. Instead, they mirrored the state's tactics. They used jurisdictional excuses and fabricated timelines to avoid investigation.

In one instance, the OCR dismissed the complaint and deferred to the PHRC while promising to review the PHRC's final decision. However, the agency declined to uphold this promise when the family contacted them within the prescribed deadline to refile the complaint with the OCR. This federal agency later dismissed the complaint when the family insisted on a fair review.

The family filed several other complaints with the OCR. But the agency either did not respond to the complaints or claimed, to our understanding, that the family's complaint was filed outside the statutory deadline, despite evidence showing it was submitted well within the required timeframe. In another instance, the OCR investigator told the family that this was a classic case of retaliation under both state and federal laws; he promised to reach back to the family for likely mediation with the university. Despite these promises, the agency remained silent and left the family in a state of limbo, as they did not know what the status of their complaint with the OCR was despite many inquiries about the status of the investigation.

The OCR, the only federal guardrail against discrimination at the state level, abdicated its duty to uphold the law and to hold academic institutions accountable, even when they initially admitted that the law was broken in this case. They, like the PHRC, the PDE, and the Attorney General's Office, among others, ignored the evidence the family presented in support of the university. This dereliction of duty and the flagrant rejection of valid information further indicated a troubling pattern within these agencies. The SPPO, for instance, tasked with protecting student privacy, ignored documented instances of Penn State's unauthorized disclosure of Ms. Oliver's academic records and their refusal to correct false information in Ms. Oliver's academic record. They cited "insufficient evidence" without reviewing the provided materials.

These failures were not oversights but deliberate choices. They reflect a stunning reality. Neither state nor federal agencies ever intended to resolve this case. In fact, it became apparent that there was a clear state agenda of containment and suppression. The Oliver-Johnson family's experience highlights a broader concern about the effectiveness of oversight in protecting civil rights and privacy. These actions raise questions about account-ability within federal agencies and their commitment to upholding the law.

The overarching theme echoed through the family's harrowing experience with federal oversight bodies like the OCR and the SPPO is the alarming inadequacy and indifference of institutions that are supposed to safeguard civil rights in the educational sphere. The overt failures of these agencies to act, despite clear evidence of wrongdoing, not only leave individuals disenfranchised but also weaken the entire structure designed to promote justice within our educational system. This scenario is emblematic of a systemic issue where bureaucratic mechanisms intended to protect civil rights devolve into tools of avoidance, effectively endorsing the very injustices they are meant to combat. The Oliver-Johnson family's struggle is a painful testament to the cascading effects of unaccountable governance, where the aspirations for equitable education and privacy rights are relegated to mere lip service.

As we transition to the next chapter, it becomes evident that the role of law enforcement as enforcers of intimidation further complicates these issues. Their involvement, or lack thereof, can not only amplify the silence surrounding such injustices but also impose an atmosphere of fear that can stifle advocacy and, ultimately, the pursuit of civil rights in education. This interplay between legal authority and civil rights warrants critical examination, as the consequences of these dynamics can profoundly impact countless students and their families.

6

THE ENFORCERS OF INTIMIDATION

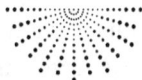

The Role of Law Enforcement as Enforcers of Intimidation

The very fabric of our civil rights in education in Pennsylvania is threatened by the insidious nature of corruption, particularly as it intersects with law enforcement. Rather than serving as protectors of justice and equality, some members of law enforcement have transformed into enforcers of intimidation, perpetuating a culture that stifles dissent and silences those who dare to speak against systemic injustices.

Schools often become battlegrounds where wealth and privilege dictate access to quality education, while marginalized communities face undue scrutiny and harassment from law enforcement, reinforcing a cycle of fear and oppression. This corruption undermines the foundational principle that every child, regardless of their background, deserves an equal opportunity to learn and thrive. As advocates for civil rights, we must confront this alarming trend head-on. They demand accountability and transparency to ensure that education becomes a true sanctuary for all, free from the taint of intimidation and corruption.

In the Oliver-Johnson case, law enforcement officials became enforcers of intimidation. In examining the chilling dynamics surrounding the family in Elizabethtown, Pennsylvania, it becomes clear that the local police, far from acting as impartial guardians of the law, have increasingly operated as enforcers of a corrupt system aimed at silencing dissent. Their interventions, draped in the guise of routine policing, have frequently coincided with the family's legal pursuits and advocacy efforts. This creates a disturbing pattern that raises fundamental questions about the integrity and accountability of law enforcement in the area.

Through a series of calculated and provocative police visits, the family has been subjected to a campaign of intimidation that seeks to undermine their advocacy. These incidents often rely on falsified or dubious claims, further illustrating the troubling state of law enforcement in the community. The actions taken against the family not only serve to reinforce the power dynamics at play but also highlight the vulnerabilities individuals face when standing up against systemic injustices.

Beyond these alarming encounters with law enforcement, the family encountered a persistent and invasive form of surveillance designed to instill fear and diminish their resolve. This insidious harassment has included the presence of unmarked vehicles near their home, which signals that their every move is under scrutiny. The intimidation tactics serve to wear down the family's spirit, which makes them feel constantly watched and vulnerable.

NEIGHBOR HARASSMENT

Neighbors, some with ties to local municipal employees, were co-opted into a campaign of harassment. These neighbors report the family to local authorities for things they are not even aware of. They reported the family for supposed minor infractions like grass height or trash placement. Violations, if they took place at all, were selectively enforced against them alone.

Neighbors fabricated trivial violations to justify authority involvement, while ignoring similar infractions committed by others. This selective reporting created a hostile environment, which further isolated the family and complicated their attempts to seek justice. It was as if they were being targeted for simply standing up for their rights, which led to a sense of deep injustice.

These petty sanctions were accompanied by more insidious tactics. They included tampered mailboxes, refused trash pick-ups, and anonymous threatening calls. Each of these actions served to heighten the family's sense of vulnerability in their own neighborhood. The cumulative effect was a psychological assault, intended to isolate the family and erode their resilience over time.

Compounding these threats, neighbors, often with affiliations to local government or hate groups, displayed hate symbols, such as Confederate flags and "Don't Tread on Me" flags, symbols, and logos, to name a few, designed to harass and intimidate the family. These neighbors have been recruited to participate in a covert campaign of bullying and terrorization against the family.

Together, these tactics amounted to a relentless psychological assault, which left the family isolated and eroded their ability to continue their fight for justice. The cumulative impact of this harassment fostered an atmosphere fraught with fear and hostility. This situation deeply challenged their resilience as they navigated the complexities of their struggles.

SUSPICIOUS POLICE ACTIVITY

Local police forces, ostensibly independent, emerged as enforcers of the corruption machine's agenda. Over the past two decades, the family has endured repeated police visits to their Elizabethtown home, each under flimsy or outright false pretenses. These visits often coincided with critical moments in The Oliver-

Johnson family's legal and advocacy efforts, such as the filing of complaints with the PHRC or public statements exposing Penn State's misconduct in 2024.

In one chilling incident in May 2024, a 911 call was claimed to have been logged from the family's home, which prompted a police response. Yet, no one in the household had made the call. This incident exemplified the distressing reality they faced, as a similar incident occurred in 2015 in which the family was detained in their own home for nearly one hour while the home was under police control and no one could leave the premises.

The 2024 incident was even more insidious. Upon arrival, police officers left their vehicles parked at a distance. They walked toward the property via alternate routes. They marked down the license plates of all the vehicles on the property; they walked around the property; they banged on the family's front door violently without announcing themselves as police officers.

The police presence at their family's home was not a random error but a calculated act of intimidation, designed to unnerve the family and signal that their actions were being monitored. Each visit and incident contributed to a pervasive atmosphere of fear and control that hindered their fight for justice.

Beyond physical visits, the family faced relentless surveillance and harassment. Unmarked vehicles were observed lingering near their property, particularly during periods of heightened advocacy. This constant scrutiny created an atmosphere of fear and anxiety for the family, which made them feel as though they were always being watched.

This series of harrowing incidents underscores a concerning intersection between civil rights and education, bringing to light how intimidation tactics can stifle advocacy and suppress dissent. The Oliver-Johnson family's experience reveals a broader systemic issue: police forces misused as tools for oppression, silencing those who aim to challenge injustices within educational institutions. By infringing upon their right to advocate for fair treatment and accountability, these methods threaten the very foundation of civil rights that protect individuals seeking change. This situation not only erodes trust in law enforcement but also reveals the chilling reality that the quest for justice in education is often met with resistance and hostility.

As the family navigates this oppressive landscape, their struggle symbolizes the fight for educational equity and civil rights across the nation. Their experience serves as a catalyst for broader discussions on the need for reform in both policing and educational systems to ensure that the voices of those advocating for change are not silenced by intimidation.

The road ahead is daunting, requiring not only courage but also solidarity among communities dedicated to preserving their rights. Yet, this battle occurs within a larger framework of information warfare and societal manipulation, the very forces that seek to bury inconvenient truths about injustices.

As we transition into the next chapter, "Digital and Social Suppression to Silence the Truth," we will explore how technology can be wielded as a double-edged sword, both empowering advocates and simultaneously serving as another mechanism of control. Here, we will unpack the challenges posed by digital censorship and the ways in which activists are finding innovative strategies to reclaim their narrative in the face of adversity.

7

DIGITAL AND SOCIAL SUPPRESSION TO SILENCE THE TRUTH

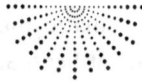

Digital and Social Suppression to Silence the Truth

A troubling wave of digital and social suppression in Pennsylvania casts a shadow over the civil rights of students in education, silencing truths that deserve to be heard. The proliferation of corrupt practices undermines the integrity of our educational institutions, where the voices of marginalized communities are stifled by bureaucratic red tape and systemic inequities. When the truth about disparities in educational resources and opportunities is systematically buried, we are not just robbing students of their rights; we are robbing future generations of the chance for equitable learning experiences.

This culture of oppression fosters an environment where transparency is a distant ideal, and accountability is traded for complacency. It is imperative that we rise against this corruption, championing a movement that demands not only access to education but the affirmation of the civil rights that should be inherent to every student in Pennsylvania. We must unite to challenge the forces that seek to silence our voices and to reclaim the narrative. We must ensure that all students, regardless of creed or individual characteristics, can pursue their dreams in an educational landscape that truly reflects fairness and equality.

In today's digital landscape, the mechanisms of communication and advocacy can often be co-opted or manipulated in ways that undermine transparency and hinder the pursuit of justice. This section delves into the challenges faced by the Oliver-Johnson family in advocating accountability, which highlight their experiences with systematic digital interference as they sought to expose misconduct at Penn State. The struggle faced by this family illustrates broader issues affecting many advocates seeking justice in similar contexts.

Far beyond mere technical issues, these disruptions appeared to be deliberate efforts to silence dissent and obscure the truth. Such actions reflect a deeper struggle between grassroots advocates and powerful institutions determined to control the narrative. The implications of these efforts are significant. They impact not only the family's pursuit of accountability but also on the larger movement for transparency.

Through the Oliver-Johnson family's account, we observe the complexities of public discourse in an age increasingly defined by social media dynamics. In this digital environment, the ability to share critical information is often at the mercy of unseen forces. This reality underscores the importance of understanding the intricate relationship between technology, advocacy, and the pursuit of justice.

COORDINATED DIGITAL INTERFERENCE

As the family escalated their case through public advocacy, they encountered systematic digital interference. Their social media accounts, used to share evidence and rally support, were throttled, shadow banned, or flagged for unspecified violations. Posts detailing Penn State's misconduct mysteriously failed to gain traction, while views supporting the university or downplaying the family's claims proliferated.

In one instance (April 28, 2025), X (Twitter)[i] blocked and later suspended the family's account sharing the truth about their ordeal. Information supported by scanned documents had been removed within hours for supposed "policy violations," despite containing no prohibited content. However, the social media platform initially restored the account a few hours later, stating that its investigation did not find that the account had disseminated spam or violated any rules. This type of censorship was frustrating for the family, who felt unjustly targeted, as their voices were being silenced unfairly and to support the university and its allies.

The family struggled to understand how legitimate evidence could be dismissed so easily in favor of narratives that protected the institution. Twitter targeted the family once more. On August 17, 2925, the family's Twitter account was suspended permanently, nearly one month after they reached out to the Haitian community on Twitter, seeking help soon after their son, Wolden, had been detained and tortured at Fort Jackson, South Carolina, while reporting for training.

Wolden had enlisted in the Army reserve and was supposed to begin training on July 28, 2025. However, on July 25, 2025, the young man had been targeted and held in a cold room without food and water for three weeks and under extreme conditions, including being deprived of basis needs, such as hygiene and communication with the outside world. The young man had been beaten and humiliated.

While in Army custody, Wolden was repeatedly told about his parents' arrogance for daring to challenge Penn State and the PHRC. They tried to entrap him by taking to the local hospital and hoping that he would escape. When he remained seated, hospital staff pressured him to leave under the threat of calling the police for trespassing. Wolden was searched several times and his person violated, as they forced needles into his finger, supposedly for medical purposes.

Upon learning about Wolden's detention at the army base, the family reached out to state officials seeking help. The family posted help-related messages on the platform, seeking assistance from others in their native tongue (Creole). But Twitter accused the family of violating their policy. Just as they claimed before (April 2025) and later retracted, Twitter claimed that the account disseminated spams and engaged in "inauthentic behavior."

The family experienced suspicious data failures, corrupted files, hacked email accounts, and disrupted internet access, which coincided with deadlines for legal submissions. This was not merely a series of unfortunate technical glitches; it felt like a coordinated effort to suppress their voice and limit their reach. Each incident heightened their suspicion of a broader campaign to undermine their advocacy efforts.

A BROADER CAMPAIGN OF NARRATIVE CONTROL

The digital suppression was part of a broader campaign to control the narrative in favor of Penn State and its allies. Local media outlets, reliant on university funding or state advertising, either ignored the family's story or published sanitized versions that omitted key details. This lack of coverage created a significant barrier for the family in sharing their experiences and truths.

The family suspected that public relations firms, [likely] contracted by Penn State or state agencies, flooded online platforms with dismissive comments or polished statements framing the university as a victim of "baseless accusations." Google, as an internet giant, also engaged in what seemed like a defensive campaign to portray the university involved in the case as victims, while undermining the family's advocacy. The family's official website (justiceformyfamily2025.com) was throttled to suppress the truth.

Statements exonerating the university had been shared within close circles. They were seemingly disseminated widely, which contributed to a distorted public perception of the situation. The campaign extended to academic circles, where scholars sympathetic to the family's cause faced pressure to retract their support or risk professional repercussions.

The corruption machine's ability to shape public perception underscores its reach and sophistication. No law firm would consider the family's request for representation. In one instance, one law firm made it clear that it would not represent the family and suggested that their claims against the university and state agencies were frivolous, which did not even warrant any attention on the part of the firm. Other law firms simply did not even acknowledge their plea for legal representation.

Civil rights agencies, notably the ACLUPA (American Civil Liberties Union for Pennsylvania[ii]), FIRE (Foundation for Individual Rights and Expression[iii]), and the NAACP (National Association for the Advancement of Colored People[iv]), to name a few, had been contacted numerous times. The NAACP, for instance, often plays a pivotal role in advocating for civil rights legislation, engaging in legal challenges against discriminatory practices, and raising public awareness about racial injustice. Through grassroots organizing, education, and legal action, the NAACP seeks to ensure political, educational, social, and economic equality for all people, working to dismantle systemic racism and promote equity in society. Here, no one wanted to help the family.

The Oliver-Johnson family desperately sought legal help from the noted organisation. But these agencies, given the political implications in this instance, declined to help the family with an utmost disdain. They used vague excuses, such as lack of resources or issues that do not rise to the level of advocacy, which they are engaged in at the grassroots level.

The sad reality is that the ACLUPA is known their its active participation in civil rights issues across the state. The agency often engages in various activities including litigation, advocacy, and public education to address issues such as free speech, privacy, equality, and criminal justice reform, working to ensure that the civil rights of all Pennsylvanians are protected and upheld. However, for the Oliver-Johnson family, the silence was revealing. It became evident that these agencies have been captured by political interests in this case.

This series of rejections and the mounting pressure from the university created a sense of vulnerability and powerlessness. It became evident that the family had been targeted by powerful entities, not only at the local level but also at both the state and federal levels. This reality created a chilling effect, which announced a very dire future for them if they remained silent.

The deliberate manipulation of information about the case ensures that the family's truth struggles to break through the noise. Their story remains largely unheard. It was overshadowed by the powerful narrative pushed by the institution and its allies at distinct levels, which include local, state, and federal.

As this family's desperate fight for civil rights within the educational system highlights, the struggle against systemic injustices is compounded by the overwhelming force of narrative control. When the institutions that are supposed to serve and protect individuals instead become the architects of their silencing, we witness a chilling effect not only on those who seek justice but also on the fundamental principles of free expression and inquiry in education. The deliberate obstruction of the family's story underscores a disturbing truth: civil rights are not merely legal protection but a battleground over the stories that shape our collective understanding and culture. The suppression of dissent and the prioritization of institutional narratives can create environments where fear stifles advocacy and erases far-reaching consequences for civil rights, especially in educational contexts.

> By advocating for freedom of speech, due process, and individual rights on college campuses and beyond, FIRE aims to protect the principles of open discourse and diverse viewpoints, standing against censorship and punitive measures against those who exercise their right to speak. Through legal advocacy, education, and public outreach, FIRE seeks to foster an environment where free expression is valued and upheld.

It is imperative that we recognize and resist the mechanisms that perpetuate these injustices. We must strive to champion transparency and accountability within educational institutions. The voices of those marginalized by the corruption machine must be amplified as they seek to reclaim their narratives and assert their rights. As we turn our focus forward, we must delve into the mechanics of the corruption machine. We must explore the intricate networks that sustain these abuses and how they impact civil rights within our educational frameworks.

---

i. X, formerly known as Twitter, is a social media platform that enables users to share short messages, known as tweets, which can include text, images, videos, and links. Founded by Jack Dorsey, Biz Stone, Evan Williams, and Noah Glass in 2006, it became a prominent channel for real-time news, social interaction, and public discourse. In 2022, Elon Musk acquired Twitter and rebranded it as X, signifying a broader vision to transform the platform into an "everything app," expanding its functionalities beyond microblogging to incorporate various services like social networking, payments, and more. The rebranding aims to reflect a shift towards more diverse and expansive features, positioning the platform as a versatile hub for communication and commerce.

ii. ACLUPA stands for the American Civil Liberties Union of Pennsylvania, which is a state affiliate of the National American Civil Liberties Union (ACLU). The organization is dedicated to defending and advancing individual rights and liberties as guaranteed by the U.S. Constitution and Pennsylvania's laws.

iii. The Foundation for Individual Rights and Expression (FIRE) is a nonprofit organization dedicated to defending and promoting the rights of individuals to express themselves freely, particularly in academic and public settings.

iv. The NAACP, or National Association for the Advancement of Colored People, is a civil rights organization founded in 1909 aimed at addressing and combating racial discrimination and promoting social justice for African Americans and other marginalized groups.

8

THE MECHANICS OF THE CORRUPTION MACHINE

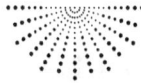

I n examining the complex dynamics of systemic corruption, the concept of "Interlocking Complicity" reveals how various institutions collaborate to maintain an oppressive status quo. Entities such as Penn State, the Pennsylvania Human Relations Commission (PHRC), law enforcement, local municipalities, and federal agencies function like interconnected gears in a machine, with no single part bearing the full brunt of accountability. This creates a robust system that effectively protects its members from facing consequences for their actions.

When misconduct at Penn State is unveiled, the PHRC swiftly dismisses complaints to shield the university from repercussions. This action exemplifies how interconnected institutions work together to sustain an environment of impunity. On occasions when their failures are brought to light, federal agencies, like the Office for Civil Rights (OCR), step in to provide a veneer of legitimacy.

This intricate network of deflection ensures that while the system collectively perpetuates injustice, it can claim plausible deniability. The collaboration among these entities stifles those who challenge the corruption machine's integrity. Thus, individuals seeking accountability often face insurmountable barriers due to this systemic interdependence among various governmental entities, many of whom had been designed to foster transparency and accountability.

COUNTERING ACCOUNTABILITY DEMANDS

The machine's strategies include a range of tools designed to wear down those who dare to resist, which embody a methodology rooted in attrition. With bureaucratic delays that prolong processes indefinitely and procedural barriers that siphon time and resources, the targeted families find themselves in an exhausting struggle against the very institutions meant to protect them. This ongoing battle against a [seemingly] indifferent system drains the families of their energy and resolve over time.

Retaliation surfaces through intimidation by law enforcement, professional ostracism, and even invasive actions against the family's children, which illustrates a calculated approach to silence dissent. These tactics create an environment of fear, which makes it increasingly difficult for families to assert their rights or seek help. As the pressure mounts, many victims feel compelled to remain silent, further entrenching the cycle of oppression.

The most chilling aspect of this corruption machine is its strategic silence. It manifests as a refusal to engage with substantiated evidence, effectively suffocating truth and leaving the victims isolated in their fight for justice. This lack of response serves to reinforce the notion that challenging the system is futile, which contributes to a sense of hopelessness among the affected families.

This orchestrated indifference not only reinforces the cycle of oppression but firmly inhibits the possibility of any meaningful resolution. Over time, the absence of accountability allows the corrupt mechanisms to thrive, which ensures that the suffering of those targeted remains unacknowledged. In this environment, the struggle for justice becomes an uphill battle, with little hope for change or recovery.

INTERLOCKING COMPLICITY

The corruption machine's power lies in its interlocking structure. Each entity, Penn State, PHRC, police, municipalities, and federal agencies, operates as a cog, with no single body bearing the full weight of responsibility. This division of labor ensures plausible deniability: no one entity can be held solely accountable. Yet, they all contribute to the system's equilibrium.

When Penn State's misconduct is exposed, the PHRC steps in to dismiss complaints. When the PHRC's failures are challenged, federal agencies like the OCR provide cover. This creates a cycle where each entity protects the other. This allows corruption to persist without repercussion.

When the family seeks public support, police and municipal harassment intensifies, while digital suppression limits their reach. The machine's goal is not to deliver justice or uncover the truth but to contain the threat posed by the family's persistence. In this way, the structure is designed to maintain control and silence dissent, which ensures that the corruption continues unchallenged.

TOOLS OF ATTRITION

The machine employs a range of tools to wear down its targets. Delays are a primary weapon: complaints languish in bureaucratic limbo, with agencies issuing vague responses or requesting redundant documentation. Procedural rabbit holes, such as the PHRC's Power of Attorney requirements, force the family to expend time, money, and energy navigating invented obstacles.

Retaliation is another tool. It is manifested as police intimidation, professional blacklisting, and attacks on the family's children. These attacks include strip-searching their eldest son and false accusations against others. Such tactics are not reactive but proactive; they are designed to discourage exposure and exhaust the family's resolve.

The machine thrives on attrition. They bet that their victims will eventually relent under the weight of sustained pressure. Its mechanisms are in place to ensure that the family does not feel overwhelmed. The relentless nature of these tactics makes it incredibly difficult for them to seek justice or support.

STRATEGIC SILENCE

Perhaps the most insidious feature of the corruption machine is its reliance on strategic silence. When confronted with evidence, letters, recordings, policy documents, the implicated agencies do not engage or refute; they simply ignore. This silence is not passive but active, a calculated strategy to starve the family's claims of oxygen.

Penn State's false submissions to the PHRC were never corrected, despite being disproven. The PHRC's failure to investigate was never explained. The OCR's dismissal of valid complaints was never justified, which left the family without any formal acknowledgment of their grievances.

By refusing to acknowledge wrongdoing, the machine ensures that the truth remains buried. Meanwhile, the family's cries for justice are dismissed as unverified or exaggerated. This creates an environment where accountability is absent, and the families affected are left in despair.

In this climate of strategic silence, the implications for civil rights in education become alarmingly clear. Families seeking justice are not merely confronting the barriers of bureaucracy; they are facing a system designed to perpetuate inequality through inaction.

The callous disregard of grievances undermines the foundational principles of civil rights, access to education, equity, and accountability. The lack of engagement from authorities not only silences individual voices but also reinforces a culture of impunity where systemic injustices can flourish unchecked. For families navigating these treacherous waters, the stakes are high; their quest for educational equity[1] becomes a battle not just for their children's future, but for the very integrity of the educational system itself.

> Educational equity emphasizes the need to address systemic barriers and biases that can lead to unequal outcomes, striving to provide tailored assistance to those who may require it to achieve comparable success. In essence, educational equity seeks to create an inclusive environment where every student has the potential to thrive and reach their full capabilities.

As we shift our focus to the subsequent chapter, we will explore how family resistance to these entrenched corrupt practices emerges as a crucial force for change. Here, we will examine the role that familial advocacy plays in challenging the status quo. We will examine how these resilient voices can illuminate the path toward genuine reform.

---

1. Educational equity refers to the principle of fairness in education, ensuring that all individuals have access to the same high-quality educational opportunities, resources, and support, regardless of their background, socioeconomic status, race, gender, or any other characteristic.

9

FAMILY RESISTANCE AS A THREAT TO CORRUPTION

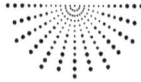

Amidst the bustling corridors of power in Pennsylvania, an immigrant family's courageous resistance emerges as a formidable challenge to the entrenched machine of corruption that threatens the sanctity of civil rights in education. This family, driven by a passionate belief in equality and justice, stands as a beacon of hope against a system that too often prioritizes political gain over the educational needs of children. Their struggle unveils the pervasive inequalities and injustices that linger in the state's schools, where resources are misallocated and opportunities are squandered due to favoritism and nepotism.

By sharing their stories of adversity and rallying their community, they shine a spotlight on the systemic failures that deny students, particularly those from marginalized backgrounds, their right to a quality education. In doing so, they challenge not only the status quo but also inspire others to rise. They demand accountability and transparency in a system that has long been shrouded in deceit. Indeed, this family's resistance is not just a personal fight; it is a clarion call for reform, justice, and a brighter future for every child in Pennsylvania. They seek to ignite a movement that threatens to dismantle the corrupt structures that have persisted for far too long.

In the face of systemic corruption and institutional indifference, the family's unwavering commitment to thorough documentation serves as both a shield and a sword. For over two decades, they have meticulously cataloged their experiences. They have built a substantial archive that goes beyond mere anecdotes to present a formidable case against a machine designed to suppress dissent. Each piece of evidence, emails, legal documents, police records, audiotapes, and photographs, not only substantiates their claims but also offers a glimpse into the inner workings of a system that seeks to silence them.

This repository of truth stands as a testament to their struggle. It is punctuated by a stark 2023 email from a PHRC official that inadvertently corroborates their assertion of neglect. Such instances not only reinforce the family's position but also draw attention to the inconsistencies in the agency's public narrative. The documentation they have collected serves multiple purposes, which ensures that their plight is not rendered invisible.

Faced with overwhelming personal costs, the family has taken their fight public. They have used social media, community engagement, and various media outlets to amplify their story. This public advocacy is more than a quest for justice; it is an act of courage that has led to tangible repercussions, which include professional isolation and unjust accusations against their children, notably the torture of their son, Wolden, by the US Army (Fort Jackson) between July 25, 2025, and August 14, 2025.

Despite facing retaliation and relentless harassment, the family remains undeterred. They are motivated by a profound sense of responsibility to unveil the truth and call for accountability. Their relentless efforts aim not only at securing justice for themselves but also at inspiring others who may find themselves entangled in a similar web of corruption and denial.

UNYIELDING DOCUMENTATION

The Oliver-Johnson family's greatest weapon against the Pennsylvania corruption machine is their relentless documentation. Over two decades, they have amassed a formidable archive: emails, legal filings, police reports, audio recordings, and photographs that chronicle every instance of abuse, harassment, and institutional failure. This evidence is not anecdotal but concrete, with time-stamps, signatures, and official letterheads that expose the machine's inner workings.

A 2024 conversation with a PHRC official reveals an insidious plot to deny the Oliver-Johnson family justice. An investigator from the PHRC (Michael Hale) inadvertently admits [on the record] to dismissing the family's complaint without review. This statement contradicted the agency's public stance that it thoroughly investigated the complaints, notably the issues they raised.

The noted record poses a direct threat to the corruption machine. They pierce its veil of deniability and invite external scrutiny. The family believes more than ever that by compiling this extensive documentation, they can hold the corrupt system accountable. They can seek justice in their plight.

PUBLIC ADVOCACY AND ESCALATION

Beyond documentation, the family has pursued public advocacy, using platforms like X, community forums, and direct appeals to journalists to share their stories. However, many of the journalists contacted have turned a blind eye to the issue, suggesting complicity or a dereliction of their journalist duties to benefit Penn State and its allies. Each individual that has been strategically contacted, each public statement, or each shared document, chips away at the machine's facade. This effort aims not only to shed light on their situation but also to seek justice and support from the community.

This advocacy has also come at a cost. The family's eldest son, Wood Oliver, was blocked from continuing his education after speaking out, while their younger children, Chandler, faced false accusations of violence and plagiarism, and Wolden, who was detained and tortured for several weeks at the Fort Jackson military base after reporting for training on July 25, 2025, the same day the PHRC attacked the family in a well-coordinated effort to intimidate and silent their complaint Penn State and their allies, which constitute rational acts of retaliation against the family for engaging in protected activities. These retaliatory actions highlight the risks involved in their quest for justice and the lengths to which some will go to silence dissent.

The parents have been targeted as well. The father, Dr. Johnson, a highly educated professional, remains blacklisted[1] for employment in Pennsylvania, while the mother, Ms. Oliver, faces ongoing digital harassment and doxing. Despite these challenges, the family has remained steadfast in its resolve.

> Being blacklisted can have serious consequences, such as hindering one's ability to secure employment, access to financial services, or participate in various activities. This practice is often used in various fields, including finance, employment, and online platforms, to protect interests or maintain security.

Yet, the family persists in their quest for justice. They are driven by a moral imperative to expose the truth and demand accountability. Their determination is a testament to their courage and the importance of their cause. They continue to

---

1. The term "blacklisted" refers to the practice of creating a list of individuals, organizations, or entities that are to be avoided, rejected, or excluded from certain privileges, services, or opportunities due to perceived misconduct, undesirable behavior, or for being deemed a risk.

believe that sharing their story can inspire others and bring about change.

The fight for civil rights in education is far from over, and the Johnson family serves as a poignant reminder of the systemic challenges that various citizens face when they dare to speak the truth. Their experience illustrates the critical intersection of advocacy and educational equity, where voices of dissent are often met with fierce retaliation rather than constructive dialogue. Retaliation not only silences individuals but also stifles the collective call for reform; it is embedded in a culture of fear that undermines the very foundations of civil rights.

As the Johnsons navigate this treacherous landscape, their story raises essential questions: How various others suffer in silence? How are they discouraged by the potential fallout of standing up? What are the broader implications for communities striving toward educational equality when those in power resort to intimidation tactics? It is a clarion call for justice. It urges society to re-evaluate the protection afforded by those who advocate for change within academic institutions.

In reflecting on these issues, we recognize that the fight for justice in education is an ongoing battle, one that requires resilience and collective action. As we transition into the next chapter, "The Machine's Design," we will delve deeper into the structural complexities that perpetuate these injustices. We will explore the systemic barriers embedded within the educational system that not only hinder progress but also define the broader societal landscape.

10

THE MACHINE'S DESIGN

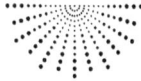

The Pennsylvania corruption machine is built to survive on its own and for its own purposes. In examining Pennsylvania's intricate web of corruption, it becomes clear that what may appear to be a malfunctioning system is, in fact, operating with chilling efficiency. The mechanisms of institutional power are designed not for the delivery of justice, but for the preservation of the status quo, effectively shielding powerful entities from accountability while stifling dissent. This observation highlights the deeply rooted issues within the system that perpetuate its dysfunction.

The case of the Oliver-Johnson family, which is at the heart of this compilation, is emblematic of a far more pervasive issue. It illustrates how every delay and every act of intimidation can be strategically employed to reinforce a system which thrives on impunity. This family's experience serves as a microcosm of the broader corruption; it showcases how personal struggles are often intertwined with systemic failures. Their plight underscores the urgent need for reform and accountability within institutions that are supposed to protect citizens.

As layers of protective measures are inserted in place, the

cycle of complicity among oversight bodies becomes apparent. This complicity raises critical questions about the integrity of institutions that claim to advocate for the vulnerable. It challenges the public's trust in the very systems that are meant to serve justice and uphold democratic values.

Ms. Oliver's story is not just an isolated incident; it represents a symptomatic failure that reverberates throughout various systems across the United States. Marginalized communities, particularly people of color and immigrant families, routinely encounter similar patterns of institutional neglect and abuse. The very bodies established to provide oversight instead align with the powerful to suppress legitimate grievances.

The nature of Pennsylvania's corruption machine exemplifies this dynamic. Its brazen tactics reflect a broader cultural malaise that questions the very foundations of democracy. Such corruption creates a culture of fear and distrust, where those in power use their political wit and administrative leverage, which may also stem from the very governmental entity designed to protect student rights, to manipulate the system to their advantage or to benefit their patrons. This situation perpetuates the cycle of injustice, which often leaves marginalized groups even more vulnerable.

The realities faced by the Oliver-Johnson family in this case compel us to confront a haunting truth: if those with well-documented claims can be so thoroughly silenced, what hope remains for those who lack the resources or platforms to make their voices heard? It is imperative to recognize that systemic failure affects not only individuals but entire communities. We must advocate for justice and demand accountability to build a more equitable system for everyone.

NOT MALFUNCTIONING, BUT THRIVING

The most chilling aspect of Pennsylvania's corruption machine is that it is not malfunctioning; it is working exactly as intended. Its purpose is not to deliver justice but to protect power. Every delay, every false report, and every act of intimidation serve to maintain the status quo.

This reality ensures that institutions like Penn State remain untouchable, while agencies like the PHRC and OCR preserve their reputations. The machine is built to survive exposure. It includes layers of redundancy and mutual protection that make accountability impossible. These mechanisms work together to create a system that benefits only those in power.

Even when evidence is presented, the machine's components close ranks, deflecting blame and neutralizing threats before they can gain traction. This creates an environment where whistle-blowers are silenced, and the truth is often obscured. The chilling reality is that this has become a normalized part of Pennsylvania's governance. This is sadly an irreconcilable verity under Josh Shapiro's administration.

A BROADER SYSTEMIC FAILURE

The Oliver-Johnson case is not an anomaly but a symptom of a broader systemic failure. Across the United States, marginalized communities, particularly Black and immigrant families, face similar patterns of institutional abuse. They are not represented. Oversight bodies collude with powerful entities to suppress dissent. There is no justice. The MLK dream ("I have a dream") is dead.

> MLK's dream refers to the vision articulated by Dr. Martin Luther King Jr. during his iconic "I Have a Dream" speech delivered in 1963. In this speech, he envisioned a racially integrated and harmonious America where individuals would be judged by their character rather than the color of their skin. His dream emphasized equality, justice, and civil rights for all people, advocating for a society free from discrimination and segregation. This vision has become a symbol of the broader struggle for civil rights and social justice, inspiring generations to work towards a more inclusive and equitable world.

In Pennsylvania, the stakes could not be higher for justice and equity. The corruption machine is brazened. Corrupt politicians are untouchable. They unashamedly leverage the state's political power and academic influence on legitimate civil rights organizations to silence critics. This must stop; this must end now.

The Oliver-Johnson family's experience raises urgent questions: If a well-documented case of civil rights violations can be so thoroughly buried, what hope is there for fewer resources victims? If agencies mandated to protect the public instead of protecting abusers, what does this say about the state of democracy?

The implications of the Oliver-Johnson case extend far beyond the immediate injustices faced by one family. They highlight a grim reality for countless marginalized communities embroiled in a system designed to perpetuate their disenfranchisement. The lack of accountability signals a dangerous precedent, one in which powerful interests can silence the voices of dissent while ignoring the fundamental rights of those they are sworn to serve. The inequity faced in education is a microcosm of larger systemic issues, where institutional neglect, coupled with collusion among oversight bodies and political elites, creates an environment ripe for exploitation.

As we confront the sobering aftermath of this case, we must illuminate the shadows in which such violations thrive. The fight for civil rights in education must not only address the isolated incidents of injustice but also challenge the deeply rooted structures that allow these violations to persist. Without sweeping reforms and a commitment to genuine equity, the dream of true justice remains hopelessly stagnant.

In laying the ground for future advocacy, we must turn our attention to the interconnectedness of these struggles. We must recognize that the fight for civil rights in education is a battle for the very soul of democracy. We must resist; we must persist in the name of justice and equity for all. We must advocate relentlessly. But we must do so in the name of fairness and social justice for all.

We stand at a critical juncture, one that calls for an unwavering commitment to redefining the narrative around civil rights in education. As we analyze the pervasive failures highlighted in the Oliver-Johnson case, we must also envision the path to a more just and equitable system. We must advocate for a system that uplifts every voice and ensures the protection of rights for all.

CONCLUSION

The Oliver-Johnson's ordeal in their quest for justice in Pennsylvania is unfathomable. But an important call to action is worthy of notes, as we conclude this book about the link between corruption and civil rights in education. There is a need to dismantle the Pennsylvania corruption machine.

There is an urgent necessity for fairness and equity in civil rights across the Commonwealth of Pennsylvania. The reason for that novel approach is simple. Vulnerable students, notably Ms. Oliver, are exposed. They are on the direct path of the Pennsylvania corruption machine.

In the heart of Pennsylvania, notably between Harrisburg and Philadelphia, the insidious grip of corruption entwines itself around our education system. This clutch stifle the civil rights of countless students and communities. It is time to shine a light on this pervasive issue and call for immediate action.

The shadowy alliances between powerful stakeholders and entrenched interests perpetuate inequities across the state. They divert resources away from those who need them most, our children, particularly in underserved and marginalized communities.

Many students are denied a quality education, which is their right. They are trapped within an archaic system that prioritizes profit over potential. This corruption undermines our foundational principles of equality and justice. They create a cycle of disenfranchisement that perpetuates poverty and limits opportunity.

We must dismantle this machine that thrives on secrecy and complicity. We must advocate for transparency, accountability, and commitment to civil rights in education. Together, we can galvanize a movement that holds our leaders accountable and ensures that every child in Pennsylvania receives the education they deserve. But it must be an education free from the poisonous influence of corruption.

The time for change is now. Our collective voice will be the catalyst for a brighter, more equitable future. We must protect student rights. We must enforce civil rights laws.

The Pennsylvania corruption machine thrives in darkness. It is sustained by silence and complicity. But it is not invincible. The Oliver-Johnson family's persistence, their refusal to be cowed, their meticulous documentation, their willingness to speak truth to power, represent a crack in the machine's armor.

To dismantle this system, external pressure is essential. Journalists must investigate, thereby shining a spotlight on Penn State's fraud and the PHRC's failures. Advocacy groups must amplify the family's voice. They must demand federal inquiries into the OCR and SPPO's inaction. Citizens must share this story, on X and beyond, to counter the machine's narrative control. Lawmakers must act; they must reform oversight mechanisms to ensure they serve the public, not the powerful.

This is not just a family fight; it is a battle for the soul of justice in Pennsylvania. The corruption machine may be formidable, but it is not unbreakable. Every shared document, every public outcry, every call for accountability weakens its grip. The question is not whether the machine can be stopped, but whether enough people will stand with the family to make it happen.

Their evidence in this case is unshakable. The Oliver-Johnson family's resolve is unbreakable. The truth is on their side. Will you join them?

ADVOCACY AND PERSECUTIONS

Here in Pennsylvania, the spirit of democracy should thrive. But there is a troubling undercurrent of corruption, which undermines the very foundations of civil rights in education. Advocacy of fair resources and fair treatment should be the norm. Yet, various educators and students find themselves persecuted for championing these essential rights. This systemic corruption stifles voices that dare to challenge the status quo. They create an environment where marginalized communities struggle to access the quality of education they deserve.

As we witness the erosion of basic civil rights, it becomes imperative for us to confront this issue head-on. We must hold accountable those who exploit their power for personal gain. By advocating for transparency and integrity within our educational institutions, we can dismantle the barriers that perpetuate inequality. We can ensure that every student in Pennsylvania has an unimpeded path to success. We can guarantee that every Pennsylvania student is free from the shadows of corruption and persecution.

After reading this book, you may still have unclear thoughts about what truly happened in the Oliver-Johnson's case. You may feel compelled to support Ms. Oliver and her family, notably me, Dr. Benjamin W. Johnson, who has had to endure this ordeal on my own. Never in my life have I faced such insurmountable obstacles.

While I am an enthusiastic individual and seldom leave family members behind, I am not a robot or a machine. I am, if it is not apparent, not an AI (The term AI is a reference to the concept known as Artificial Intelligence). I am authentic. I am a man of flesh and blood. This is not to boast. But I epitomize the proverbial David versus Goliath story, where I was no match for a powerful university, whom, when I cornered them, I felt the need to seek reinforcement from powerful entities, such as the state of Pennsylvania itself and other potent allies.

THE TRUTH SPEAKS FOR ITSELF

Throughout my ordeal, I had nothing but the truth on my side. But the assault on me was no laughing matter. Still, I have my wit, my sheer determination, and my survival instincts to survive. The university had nothing but lies to justify its conduct. Anyone who accepted the university's version of their own misconduct is because they might be a part of the ongoing assault against my family.

My involvement in the case started early. I contacted the university in August 2023 to raise concerns about the treatment that my wife, Ms. Oliver, had been subjected to, at least, by nursing school officials. While my complaints were taken seriously, at least initially, I was later subjected to a series of abuses in retaliation for my involvement in the case. I was subsequently removed from the university as an adjunct faculty; the dean of equity and diversity defamed me; I was caricatured as a violent man who needed to be restrained.

I, as a defender of the family, was targeted personally, professionally, and psychologically. The goal, as I realized, was to silence me at all costs, given my expertise in educational law and school policy and given my capacity to defend Ms. Oliver in a way that most attorneys could not, given that this case was not merely a legal issue. But there is no doubt in my mind that I was targeted in retaliation for my intervention.

I was targeted in various conversations where faculty identified me as a threat or a troublemaker, whom they had to contain by any means necessary, including involving law enforcement. In one conversation, the course instructor, Retired Army Colonel Kelly Wolgast, claimed that she could hear my voice in the background, and she would annotate that in her report to university officials. It was evident to me then and, as it is to me now, that I am a target. University officials sought to harm me as much as they could. Sadly, they are continuing to harm my family and me, notably my children.

Certainly, the university has miscalculated my resolve to resist their assault. They have similarly targeted my children, with my second child as the latest victim of their assault. However, I will not relent. I will not surrender. As I have always maintained it: this case does not end the university's way. So far, they have done enough damage to me personally and to my family to justify the need to defend myself, which might be necessary sooner rather than later, given the onslaught on me personally and on my family. In the interest of public transparency, I cannot remain silent as those in power abuse their power to the detriment of those who have no voice. I must speak. I must resist. This book you are reading now an attempt to do just that.

SUMMARY OF EVIDENCE

This book is not based on a speculative assessment of what the university has tried to frame as grading disputes while also claiming that this was not a grade dispute issue, given that the student did not request a grade adjudication before her "lawful dismissal" from Penn State. The university has unequivocally claimed that the student was dismissed based on sound academic judgement of the faculty. Yet, the university dismissed the student before the grade adjudication for the very course she supposedly failed. The university had to [at least initially] pause the dismissal to conduct what could be described as a sham grade adjudication after the student's rights had already been violated under the law.

As should be evident by now, assuming you have read the manuscript until this juncture, this case is not about academic judgment or grading disputes. Those who are a part of the Pennsylvania corruption machine have used this framing to exonerate the people involved and even to justify their own misconduct. To prove that this case was never about grading disputes, the next few pages include a series of documents, notably images, letters, and emails from school officials and others, which provide a comprehensive account of institutional misconduct, due process violations, policy manipulation [fraudulent at times], and retaliation at the *Pennsylvania State University (Penn State)*.

The evidence outlined here demonstrates how Penn State fraudulently altered its policies post-facto to justify an unlawful dismissal, rooted in the discrimination of an immigrant student by a cohort of individuals who targeted the student and sought to justify their conduct by any means necessary. The documents show how the university engaged in systematic efforts to obstruct justice. The document also reveals how other state agencies, notably the PHRC fraudulently altered official documents and mischaracterized the student's academic records to justify their own misconduct.

This case is well-documented. It is not based on conjectures about what took place here. Therefore, we challenge any statements that do not reflect the available evidence.

KEY ISSUES OUTLINED:

1. Due Process Violations— A student was dismissed without prior notice, in violation of university policies (GCAC-803), which mandate a multi-step review process.
2. Unauthorized Dismissal— The dismissal was issued by an associate dean who did not have the authority to make such a decision under university policy (GCAC-803).
3. Fraudulent Policy Changes— In July 2024, Penn State modified its policies (GCAC-803 and GCAC-401) after the fact to retroactively grant authority for the graduate student dismissal to Associate Dean Judith Hupcey, without proper disclosure.

4. Retaliation Against a Protected Individual— The dismissed student is African American, female, over 40, and an immigrant, and filed a discrimination complaint before the dismissal by one of the individuals named in the initial discrimination complaint.

5. Failure of State Agencies— The Pennsylvania Human Relations Commission (PHRC), the Office for Civil Rights (OCR), and other agencies refused to act, despite overwhelming evidence of misconduct.

6. Conflict of Interest at PHRC— The Executive Director of the PHRC received an honor from Penn State while handling the case, raising serious ethical concerns.

7. Legal Implications— The actions of Penn State officials potentially constitute fraud, obstruction of justice, and civil rights violations.

The noted documents represent snippet of the available evidence. However, this sample features primary evidence and other proofs, including the original dismissal letter (annotated), policy changes (original and modified documents), formal complaints (sample of the individuals named), and university responses to the PHRC, notably the false claims about the student request for a grade adjudication and the attorneys who echoed these falsehoods (including Attorney professional misconduct). Feel free to reach out to us for further clarifications or if you wish to see [or obtain] an actual copy of the evidence outlined in this publication.

Initially Prepared for: Attorney Review

By: Dr. Benjamin W. Johnson

Date: January 31, 2025 (Slightly updated August 2025)

DISCLAIMER

In the interest of accountability, transparency, and public interest, and considering that Penn State is a publicly funded institution, we have not redacted or altered the names and job titles of individuals mentioned in official letters, institutional policies, and electronic communications. These documents were legally obtained either as a direct recipient of these communications or as a concerned citizen seeking accountability from a public institution. Furthermore, it is our [Oliver-Johnson family] good faith understanding that the officials referenced in this matter, including those affiliated with state agencies, qualify as public figures in their professional capacity, given their roles in public education, government oversight, and administration.

DISMISSAL LETTER BY ASSOCIATE DEAN JUDITH HUPCEY (1/31/2024)

PennState
Ross and Carol Nese
College of Nursing

Ross and Carol Nese
College of Nursing
The Pennsylvania State University
201 Nursing Sciences Building
University Park, PA 16802

814-863-0245
Fax: 814-865-3779
www.nursing.psu.edu

Wednesday, January 31, 2024

Germine Oliver
P.O. Box 214
Middletown, PA 17057-0214

Dear Germine,

The Nese College of Nursing is committed to academic excellence and strives to support students in achieving academic success and preparing them to become an advanced practice nurse.

According to the Nese College of Nursing's Academic Progression Guidelines the criteria for dismissal from the nursing program states that a student receiving a grade of "B-" or lower in any two required nursing courses will face dismissal. Unfortunately, due to your unsuccessful completion of STAT 800 in the summer 2019 semester and NURS 596 in fall 2023 (which substituted for NURS 835 as per your request), a decision has been reached to terminate your enrollment in the Doctor of Nursing Practice Leadership program.

In alignment with Graduate Education Policy GCAC 401-3a, the option for a Deferred Grade (DF) was provided as an opportunity for you to complete the assigned tasks in the NURS596 course you recently attempted. Your decision to either refuse or not respond to the request to consider the DF led to the assignment of a quality grade.

Dismissal from The Nese College of Nursing program prohibits subsequent applications to any other Nese College of Nursing graduate programs. Retroactively dropped nursing course(s) do not negate unsuccessful attempts, which are tracked by the Ross and Carol Nese College of Nursing. If you have questions, please review the Academic Progression Guidelines in the student handbook on the Nese College of Nursing website at https://www.nursing.psu.edu/student-handbooks/.

You are required to change your major before the beginning of the following semester. Engaging in a program that aligns with your interests and capitalizes on your skills offers the optimal path to success. I strongly advise you to schedule a meeting with the Program Director of your chosen major to explore and identify a suitable course of study.

You have the right to appeal the decision to terminate your enrollment in the DNP Leadership program by adhering to the procedures outlined in GCAC 803: Procedures for Termination of the Degree Program of a Graduate Student for Unsatisfactory Scholarship. Should you wish to seek further review of this decision, you must submit a written appeal to the program head within ten days of receiving this notice.

Nursing wishes you the best in your future endeavors at Penn State or wherever your journey takes you.

Sincerely,

Judith E. Hupcey

Judith E. Hupcey, Ed.D., CRNP, FAAN
Associate Dean for Research & Innovation
Interim Associate Dean for Graduate Education

cc: Dean
       Program Director
       Student Advisor

PennState
Ross and Carol Nese
College of Nursing

Ross and Carol Nese
College of Nursing
The Pennsylvania State University
201 Nursing Sciences Building
University Park, PA 16802

814-863-0245
Fax: 814-865-3779
www.nursing.psu.edu

Wednesday, January 31, 2024

Germine Oliver
P.O. Box 214
Middletown, PA 17057-0214

Dear Germine,

[Annotation: Student completed all required courses in the program. NURS 596 was initially a non-graded independent study course. A formal request for a grade adjudication was pending at the time the dismissal letter was issued, which constituted a violation of school policy G-10.]

[Annotation: Violates policy GCAC-803, which requires advance notice in writing and the dismissal process ends with the decision by the dean of the graduate school.]

The Nese College of Nursing is committed to academic excellence and strives to support students in achieving academic success and preparing them to become an advanced practice nurse.

According to the Nese College of Nursing's Academic Progression Guidelines the criteria for dismissal from the nursing program states that a student receiving a grade of "B-" or lower in any two required nursing courses will face dismissal. Unfortunately, due to your unsuccessful completion of STAT 800 in the summer 2019 semester and NURS 596 in fall 2023 (which substituted for NURS 835 as per your request), a decision has been reached to terminate your enrollment in the Doctor of Nursing Practice Leadership program.

[Annotation: Violates Penn State policy 47-20. Non-graded courses cannot be assigned a DF grade.]

In alignment with Graduate Education Policy GCAC 401-3a, the option for a Deferred Grade (DF) was provided as an opportunity for you to complete the assigned tasks in the NURS596 course you recently attempted. Your decision to either refuse or not respond to the request to consider the DF led to the assignment of a quality grade.

Dismissal from The Nese College of Nursing program prohibits subsequent applications to any other Nese College of Nursing graduate programs. Retroactively dropped nursing course(s) do not negate unsuccessful attempts, which are tracked by the Ross and Carol Nese College of Nursing. If you have questions, please review the Academic Progression Guidelines in the student handbook on the Nese College of Nursing website at https://www.nursing.psu.edu/student-handbooks/.

[Annotation: Violates policy GCAC-804. This is not the authority of the nursing school at this point, as the dean of the graduate school has not revoked the dismissal yet.]

You are required to change your major before the beginning of the following semester. Engaging in a program that aligns with your interests and capitalizes on your skills offers the optimal path to success. I strongly advise you to schedule a meeting with the Program Director of your chosen major to explore and identify a suitable course of study.

[Annotation: Violates student's due process rights, as the dismissal process has not begun yet.]

You have the right to appeal the decision to terminate your enrollment in the DNP Leadership program by adhering to the procedures outlined in GCAC 803: Procedures for Termination of the Degree Program of a Graduate Student for Unsatisfactory Scholarship. Should you wish to seek further review of this decision, you must submit a written appeal to the program head within ten days of receiving this notice.

[Annotation: Violates policy GCAC-803, as the student has the right to appeal the determination of the dismissal by the doctoral committee. This student has the right to appeal the decision by the program head if she were to sustain the determination by the doctoral committee after the due process was followed. The student has the right to appeal the decision by the program head, with the dean of the graduate school, whose decision on the matter is final.]

Nursing wishes you the best in your future endeavors at Penn State or wherever your journey takes you.

Sincerely,

[Annotation: Cannot say "best in your future endeavors" and also advise her to enroll in more than two other PSU programs.]

Judith E. Hupcey

Judith E. Hupcey, Ed.D., CRNP, FAAN
Associate Dean for Research & Innovation
Interim Associate Dean for Graduate Education

cc: Dean
       Program Director
       Student Advisor

[Annotation: Violates policy GCAC-803. Only a Doctoral Committee can determine that a doctoral student can be dismissed from a graduate program for poor scholarship. As the Associate Dean for Research & Innovation and the Interim Associate Dean for Graduate Education, Judith Hupcey cannot unilaterally dismiss a doctoral student and then no other school officials. This is abuse of power.]

[Annotation: Violates policy GCAC-803, as Associate Dean Judith Hupcey asserts that she is not the program head. Therefore, she does not have the authority to oversee the determination of the dismissal of a doctoral student for poor scholarship, let alone to dismiss the student unilaterally outside the scope of the established dismissal process.]

ORIGINAL-UNIVERSITY
POLICY GCAC-803/PAGE 1 (AS OF
04/23/2024)

Proof 7: GCAC-803 policy requirements for student dismissal

GCAC-803

Procedures for Termination of the Degree Program of a Graduate
Student for Unsatisfactory Scholarship

Purpose
To describe the procedure by which a graduate student is terminated from a graduate program for unsatisfactory scholarship.

Scope
All graduate students.

Policy Statement

1. Where the basis for unsatisfactory scholarship is behavior that is believed to fall within the Code of Conduct, it should first be referred to the Office of Student Conduct for adjudication. (See GCAC-801 Conduct).

    a. If the Office of Student Conduct determines that the graduate student did not engage in a Code of Conduct behavior, and if the sole basis for unsatisfactory scholarship was if the behavior did fall within the Code of Conduct, no further action should be taken.

    b. If the Office of Student Conduct determines the graduate student has engaged in a Code of Conduct behavior and issues a sanction(s), does constitute unsatisfactory scholarship and further action may be taken by the program and/or the Graduate School.

2. When a graduate program head, program committee, or, in the case of a doctoral student, the doctoral committee determines that the program of a graduate student must be terminated for unsatisfactory scholarship, the student must be given advance notice, in writing, which in general terms shall advise the student of the reasons for the termination.

    a. Examples of unsatisfactory scholarship may include, but are not limited to:

        i. failure to exhibit and promote the highest ethical, moral, and professional standards;

        ii. inadequate grade-point average;

        iii. failure to obtain satisfactory grades in required courses for the program;

        iv. failure to make satisfactory progress in research or other activities related to the culminating experience; or

        v. failing the qualifying, comprehensive, or final oral examination for doctoral students.

3. Upon receipt of this notice, the student has the opportunity to seek a review of the decision. If the student desires such a review, the student must, within ten days of receipt of the notice, submit a written appeal to the program head.

4. If the student alleges that discrimination either was the reason for the termination or caused the unsatisfactory scholarship, and the discrimination or harassment was committed by an individual in a role of authority, such as an administrator, faculty member, instructor, teaching assistant, or research assistant, the matter shall be referred to the Affirmative Action Office of the University, established to review such claim

    a. If the Affirmative Action Office determines that the student's allegation has merit, the Affirmative Action Office will manage the investigation and report back to the program head and any other University office as appropriate.

    b. If the Affirmative Action Office determines that the student's allegation is unfounded, the graduate program head then provides an opportunity for the student to meet with him/her and, if applicable, the program committee, doctoral committee, or other faculty involved in the decision to terminate the student's program.

ORIGINAL-UNIVERSITY
POLICY GCAC-803/PAGE 2 (AS OF
04/23/2024)

5. If there is no allegation of discrimination within the written appeal, then the graduate program head provides an opportunity for the student t meet with the faculty member(s) who made the decision to terminate the student's program.

   a. This meeting must be held within 30 days of receipt of the student's written appeal.

      i. Under extraordinary circumstances, either party may request a stay to the 30-day time limit. A request for such a stay must includ justification and indicate the desired duration of the stay, and be directed to the Dean of the Graduate School, whose decision on t stay will be final.

   b. Formal rules of evidence are not applicable to the meeting, and attorneys are not permitted to represent any person attending the meeting.

   c. If the student's faculty adviser would not otherwise be present (i.e., was not involved in the decision to terminate), the adviser should b permitted to attend this meeting if requested by the student or graduate program head, or if the adviser wishes to do so.

   d. The graduate program head is responsible for ensuring that minutes of the meeting are taken and copies distributed to all those in attendance.

6. Following this meeting, the graduate program head must notify the student within five days, in writing, whether the termination decision has been sustained or reversed.

   a. If it is sustained, the graduate program head shall notify the Dean of the Graduate School. If the termination is based upon failure to exhibit and promote the highest ethical, moral, and professional standards expected of graduate students, the Graduate School may als make a determination to dismiss the student from continued or future enrollment in any graduate program at the University. If the

Graduate School dismisses the student from continued or future enrollment in any graduate program at the University, notification of this decision will be given to the student within this time frame as well.

7. Within five days of receiving this notice of termination for unsatisfactory scholarship, the student may make a written request to the Dean of the Graduate School for a further review of the decision. The student is permitted to submit additional information or statements in writing.

   a. Although not required to do so, the Dean of the Graduate School may meet with the student and/or graduate program head, or request additional information from the student and/or the graduate program head. If a meeting is held, the student may not be represented by attorney, but may have present a faculty adviser of his or her choice.

   b. The standard of review by the Graduate School is whether the decision to terminate for unsatisfactory scholarship was arbitrary and capricious. The terms "arbitrary and capricious" mean that the decision to terminate is not supportable on any rational basis, or that the is no evidence upon which the decision may be based. The Graduate School does not review faculty judgments as to the quality of a student's academic performance (e.g., the quality of a thesis or dissertation, performance on a comprehensive examination, etc.), but or whether a program's decision was arbitrary and capricious, including in cases of failure to exhibit and promote the highest ethical, moral and professional standards expected of graduate students.

8. After this review, the Dean of the Graduate School either sustains the termination or, if he/she determines that the decision was arbitrary and capricious, reverses the decision with any corrective action, and permits the student to continue in the program.

   a. If the termination is sustained, the Dean of the Graduate School directs, at their discretion for termination from the Graduate School and at the discretion of the program for termination from only the graduate program in which the student is enrolled, that the termination be entered on the student's transcript.

   b. The Dean of the Graduate School gives written notice of the decision to the program head and to the student within three weeks of rece of the student's written request to the Dean.

   c. In the event of a reversal, such written notice shall contain a statement of the basis upon which the decision was made.

9. The decision by the Dean of the Graduate School is final.

ORIGINAL-UNIVERSITY
POLICY GCAC-803/PAGE 3 (AS OF
04/23/2024)

10. A registration hold may be placed on the student's records while action is pending under these procedures.

11. Nothing in this policy is intended to constitute a contract or contractual terms. No provisions of this policy shall confer contractual rights upon any parties. To the extent that this policy may be applicable to faculty or staff, the terms outlined herein do not constitute terms, benefits, or conditions of employment. The terms set forth herein are subject to change unilaterally and without notice by University administration.

Revision History

- Adapted from the Graduate Bulletin: June 2018.
- Revisions proposed by the Graduate Council Committee on Academic Standards and approved by Graduate Council, February 2013.
- Revisions by the Graduate Council Committee on Academic Standards, January 2008.
- Revised by special Ad Hoc Committee on Student-Related Policies, April 2007.
- Revised by special Ad Hoc Committee on Student-Related Policies, August 2005
- Approved by the Graduate Council, May 8, 2002.
  ○ New policy.

This page was generated on April 23, 2024 at 1:41 AM local time. This may not be the most recent version of this page. Check the Penn State Graduate School website for updates.

MODIFIED-UNIVERSITY
POLICY GCAC-803/PAGE 1 (JULY 19
2024 AND AS OF 01/25/2025)

Funding +   Student Support +   Equity +   About +   Resource Library   ☰ More

Policy Statement

1. Where the basis for unsatisfactory scholarship is behavior that is believed to fall within the Code of Conduct, it should first be referred to the Office of Student Conduct for adjudication. (See GCAC-801 Conduct).

   a. If the Office of Student Conduct determines that the graduate student did not engage in a Code of Conduct behavior, and if the sole basis for unsatisfactory scholarship was if the behavior did fall within the Code of Conduct, no further action should be taken.

   b. If the Office of Student Conduct determines the graduate student has engaged in a Code of Conduct behavior and issues a sanction(s), this does constitute unsatisfactory scholarship and further action may be taken by the program and/or the J. Jeffrey and Ann Marie Fox Graduate School.

2. When a *graduate program head*, program committee, or, in the case of a doctoral student, the doctoral committee determines that the program of a graduate student must be terminated for unsatisfactory scholarship, the student must be given advance notice, in writing, which in general terms shall advise the student of the reasons for the termination.

   a. Examples of unsatisfactory scholarship may include, but are not limited to:

      i. failure to exhibit and promote the highest ethical, moral, and professional standards;

      ii. inadequate grade-point average;

      iii. failure to obtain satisfactory grades in required courses for the program;

      iv. failure to make satisfactory progress in research or other activities related to the culminating experience; or

      v. failing the qualifying, comprehensive, or final oral examination for doctoral students.

3. Upon receipt of this notice, the student has the opportunity to seek a review of the decision. If the student desires such a review, the student must, within ten days of receipt of the notice, submit a written appeal to the program head.

4. If the student alleges that discrimination either was the reason for the termination or caused the unsatisfactory scholarship, and the discrimination or harassment was committed by an individual in a role of authority, such as an administrator, faculty member, instructor, teaching assistant, or research assistant, the matter shall be referred to the Affirmative Action Office of the University, established to review such claims.

   a. If the Affirmative Action Office determines that the student's allegation has merit, the Affirmative Action Office will manage the investigation and report back to the program head and any other University office as appropriate.

   b. If the Affirmative Action Office determines that the student's allegation is unfounded, the graduate program head then provides an opportunity for the student to meet with him/her and, if applicable, the program committee, doctoral committee, or other faculty involved in the decision to terminate the student's program.

MODIFIED-UNIVERSITY
POLICY GCAC-803/PAGE 2 (JULY 19,
2024, AND AS OF 01/25/2025)

5. If there is no allegation of discrimination within the written appeal, then the graduate program head provides an opportunity for the student to meet with the faculty member(s) who made the decision to terminate the student's program.

   a. This meeting must be held within 30 days of receipt of the student's written appeal.

      i. Under extraordinary circumstances, either party may request a stay to the 30-day time limit. A request for such a stay must include a justification and indicate the desired duration of the stay, and be directed to the Dean of the Fox Graduate School, whose decision on the stay will be final.

   b. Formal rules of evidence are not applicable to the meeting, and attorneys are not permitted to represent any person attending the meeting.

   c. If the student's faculty adviser would not otherwise be present (i.e., was not involved in the decision to terminate), the adviser should be permitted to attend this meeting if requested by the student or graduate program head, or if the adviser wishes to do so.

   d. The graduate program head is responsible for ensuring that minutes of the meeting are taken and copies distributed to all those in attendance.

6. Following this meeting, the graduate program head must notify the student within five days, in writing, whether the termination decision has been sustained or reversed.

   a. If it is sustained, the graduate program head shall notify the Dean of the Fox Graduate School. If the termination is based upon failure to exhibit and promote the highest ethical, moral, and professional standards expected of graduate students, the Fox Graduate School may also make a determination to dismiss the student from continued or future enrollment in any graduate program at the University. If the Fox Graduate School dismisses the student from continued or future enrollment in any graduate program at the University, notification of that decision will be given to the student within this time frame as well.

7. Within five days of receiving this notice of termination for unsatisfactory scholarship, the student may make a written request to the Dean of the Fox Graduate School for a further review of the decision. The student is permitted to submit additional information or statements in writing.

   a. Although not required to do so, the Dean of the Fox Graduate School may meet with the student and/or graduate program head, or request additional information from the student and/or the graduate program head. If a meeting is held, the student may not be represented by an attorney, but may have present a faculty adviser of his or her choice.

   b. The standard of review by the Fox Graduate School is whether the decision to terminate for unsatisfactory scholarship was arbitrary and capricious. The terms "arbitrary and capricious" mean that the decision to terminate is not supportable on any rational basis, or that there is no evidence upon which the decision may be based. The Fox Graduate School does not review faculty judgments as to the quality of a student's academic performance (e.g., the quality of a *thesis* or *dissertation*, performance on a comprehensive examination, etc.), but only whether a program's decision was arbitrary and capricious, including in cases of failure to exhibit and promote the highest ethical, moral, and professional standards expected of graduate students.

MODIFIED-UNIVERSITY
POLICY GCAC-803/PAGE 3 (JULY 19
2024 AND AS OF 01/25/2025)

Funding +   Student Support +   Equity +   About +   Resource Library   ≡ More

8. After this review, the Dean of the Fox Graduate School either sustains the termination or, if he/she determines that the decision was arbitrary and capricious, reverses the decision with any corrective action, and permits the student to continue in the program.

   a. If the termination is sustained, the Dean of the Fox Graduate School directs, at their discretion for termination from the Fox Graduate School and, at the discretion of the program for termination from only the graduate program in which the student is enrolled, that the termination be entered on the student's transcript.

   b. The Dean of the Fox Graduate School gives written notice of the decision to the program head and to the student within three weeks of receipt of the student's written request to the Dean.

   c. In the event of a reversal, such written notice shall contain a statement of the basis upon which the decision was made.

9. The decision by the Dean of the Fox Graduate School is final.

10. A registration hold may be placed on the student's records while action is pending under these procedures.

11. Nothing in this policy is intended to constitute a contract or contractual terms. No provisions of this policy shall confer contractual rights upon any parties. To the extent that this policy may be applicable to faculty or staff, the terms outlined herein do not constitute terms, benefits, or conditions of employment. The terms set forth herein are subject to change unilaterally and without notice by University administration.

Revision History

- Adapted from the Graduate Bulletin: June 2018.

- Revisions proposed by the Graduate Council Committee on Academic Standards and approved by Graduate Council, February 2013.

- Revisions by the Graduate Council Committee on Academic Standards, January 2008.

- Revised by special Ad Hoc Committee on Student-Related Policies, April 2007.

- Revised by special Ad Hoc Committee on Student-Related Policies, August 2005.

- Approved by the Graduate Council, May 8, 2002.

   - New policy.

- Editorial revisions to reflect the new name of the Fox Graduate School, July 19, 2024.

MODIFIED-POLICY GCAC-803/NEW PROGRAM HEAD DEFINITION (07/19/2024 AND AS OF 01/25/2025)

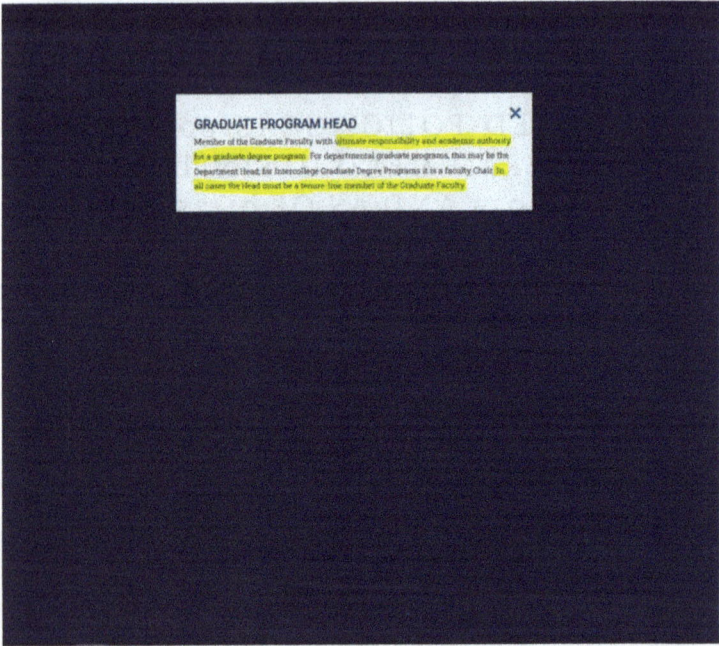

GCAC-803 POLICY REVISION
CONCEALED (AS OF 01/25/2025)

POLICY CHANGE - EFFECTIVE IMMEDIATELY

GCAC-211 Joint Degrees

Approved by Graduate Council, November 20, 2024

Effective date: November 20, 2024

- Revised to remove specific references to the J.D. and M.D. to expand eligibility to other law and medical degrees offered by the University.

NEW POLICY - EFFECTIVE FALL 2024

GCAC-218 Minors

Approved by Graduate Council, May 1, 2024

Effective date: Fall 2024 (August 12, 2024)

POLICY CHANGE - EFFECTIVE IMMEDIATELY

GCAC-212 Postbaccalaureate Credit Certificate Programs

Approved by Graduate Council, May 1, 2024

Effective date: May 1, 2024

- Policy Statement #5 revised to replace "regionally accredited" with a link to approved accreditation agencies.

POLICY CHANGE - EFFECTIVE IMMEDIATELY

GCAC-301 Qualifications for Admission

Approved by Graduate Council, May 1, 2024

Effective date: May 1, 2024

- Policy Statement #2 revised to replace "regionally accredited" with a link to approved accreditation agencies.

POLICY CHANGE - EFFECTIVE IMMEDIATELY

GCAC-305 Admission Requirements for International Students

Approved by Graduate Council, May 1, 2024

UNIVERSITY/ATTORNEY LIES (AS OF 07/15/2024)

11. Denied as stated. On February 7, 2024, Respondent informed Complainant that it would conduct a grade adjudication, despite the fact that Complainant had not requested a grade adjudication prior to her January 31, 2024, academic dismissal letter from the College of Nursing. By way of further response, Respondent informed Complainant that, pursuant to Penn State policy, she could request a Leave of Absence in order to maintain access to her Penn State email account and other amenities because Complainant had not registered for any classes for the Spring 2024 semester at that time.

Respectfully submitted,

BUCHANAN INGERSOLL & ROONEY PC

/s/ George C. Morrison
George C. Morrison, Esq. (PA 203223)
Keith M. Lee, Esq. (PA 330237)
Andrew T. Simmons, Esq. (PA 331973)
Two Liberty Place
50 S. 16th Street, Suite 3200
Philadelphia, PA 19102
(215) 665-3909

Counsel for Respondent

Dated: July 15, 2024

DUE PROCESS VIOLATION/ATTORNEY MISCONDUCT (UNIVERSITY RESPONSE TO THE PHRC ON 07/15/2024)

DUE PROCESS VIOLATIONS

FALSE STATEMENT TO A TRIBUNAL

11. Denied as stated. On February 7, 2024, Respondent informed Complainant that it would conduct a grade adjudication, despite the fact that Complainant had not requested a grade adjudication prior to her January 31, 2024, academic dismissal letter from the College of Nursing. By way of further response, Respondent informed Complainant that, pursuant to Penn State policy, she could request a Leave of Absence in order to maintain access to her Penn State email account and other amenities because Complainant had not registered for any classes for the Spring 2024 semester at that time.

Respectfully submitted,

BUCHANAN INGERSOLL & ROONEY PC

/s/ George C. Morrison
George C. Morrison, Esq. (PA 203223)
Keith M. Lee, Esq. (PA 330237)
Andrew T. Simmons, Esq. (PA 331973)
Two Liberty Place
50 S. 16th Street, Suite 3200
Philadelphia, PA 19102
(215) 665-3909

PROFESSIONAL MISCONDUCT BY THE ATTORNEYS

Dated: July 15, 2024   *Counsel for Respondent*

From: Oliver, Germine A <gobien5027@psu.edu>
Sent: Wednesday, January 24, 2024 3:28 PM
To: Hupcey, Judith E <jhupcey@psu.edu>; Badzek, Laurie <lzb340@psu.edu>; Matter, Sheri <sxm1898@psu.edu>; Wright Watson, Denita Renee <Denita@psu.edu>; Adair, Suzanne <sca917@psu.edu>; Fong, Duncan King-Hoi <i2v@psu.edu>; Grad Dean's Office <graddeansoffice@psu.edu>; Oman, Tabitha <txo5152@psu.edu>
Subject: Grade Adjudication request

Hello,

To whom it may concern.

Below is my formal request for a grade adjudication in the N596 independent study (Fall 2023).

The grade received violates school policy 47-20. The instructor did not provide a written (paper or electronic form) notification of the basis for grades to me on or before the first class meeting.

Also, I have been informed in an email correspondence by a representative from the office of Affirmative Action that I am being terminated from the nursing program for missing previously specified deadlines. This is another excuse to justify a blatant discriminatory act against my person at Penn State University. I intend to challenge these unsubstantiated claims as vigorously as Penn State policy guidelines would allow. It is my understanding that there are no such stipulations neither in school policy nor in the student handbook for the DNP program. I completed all the benchmarks and other requirements, as specified in the DNP program and within the prescribed timeline, except for the oral presentation, which is beyond my purview.

I intend to appeal any arbitrary decisions if and when they are communicated to me officially.

Please see attached document for the grade adjudication.

Germine Oliver

1/24/2024, 4:

FORMAL GRADE ADJUDICATION REQUEST (1/24/2024)

From: Oliver, Germine A <gobien5027@psu.edu>
Sent: Wednesday, January 24, 2024 3:28 PM
To: Hupcey, Judith E <jhupcey@psu.edu>; Badzek, Laurie <lzb340@psu.edu>; Matter, Sheri <sxm1898@psu.edu>; Wright Watson, Denita Renee <Denita@psu.edu>; Adair, Suzanne <sca917@psu.edu>; Fong, Duncan King-Hoi <i2v@psu.edu>; Grad Dean's Office <graddeansoffice@psu.edu>; Oman, Tabitha <txo5152@psu.edu>
Subject: Grade Adjudication request

Hello,

To whom it may concern.

Below is my formal request for a grade adjudication in the N596 independent study (Fall 2023).

The grade received violates school policy 47-20. The instructor did not provide a written (paper or electronic form) notification of the basis for grades to me on or before the first class meeting.

Also, I have been informed in an email correspondence by a representative from the office of Affirmative Action that I am being terminated from the nursing program for missing previously specified deadlines. This is another excuse to justify a blatant discriminatory act against my person at Penn State University. I intend to challenge these unsubstantiated claims as vigorously as Penn State policy guidelines would allow. It is my understanding that there are no such stipulations neither in school policy nor in the student handbook for the DNP program. I completed all the benchmarks and other requirements, as specified in the DNP program and within the prescribed timeline, except for the oral presentation, which is beyond my purview.

I intend to appeal any arbitrary decisions if and when they are communicated to me officially.

Please see attached document for the grade adjudication.

Germine Oliver

FORMAL GRADE ADJUDICATION REQUEST FORM (1/24/2024)

Grade Adjudication Petition Form

This form must be filed with the associate dean or director of academic affairs of the college or campus offering the course no later than ten weeks following the end date of the course (as it appears in the schedule of courses).

Name: _____ Germine Oliver _____   Date: ___ 1/11/24 _____

Address: ██████████████████████   Phone: __ (717) 616-5352 _____

_____   Student Number: 9████████

Course for which you believe an improper grade was assigned:

Course Name, Number and Section: N596 Individual Study _____

Semester: (Fall)   Spring   Summer   Year: _ 2023 _____

College/Campus: ____ World Campus _____

Grade received: ___ F _____   Instructor: ___ Kelly Wolgast _____

Before filing a grade adjudication petition, you must first discuss grading practices and assignments with the instructor. It is expected that the student and instructor will try to eliminate any misunderstandings and will attempt to work out any disagreements over grades. You must also request mediation by the head of the academic program offering the course. Sign your name to certify you have done this:

Certification from the instructor that you have attempted to eliminate any misunderstanding over the assigned grade:

____ Germine Oliver _____   Date: ___ 1/11/2024 _____

Certification from the head of the academic program offering the course that you have attempted to eliminate any misunderstanding over the assigned grade:

____ Germine Oliver _____   Date: ___ 1/11/2024 _____

Please explain the reasons why you believe your instructor has not followed the grading policy described in Faculty Senate Policy 47-20 or related Faculty Senate policies on grades:

The instructor did not provide a written (paper or electronic form) notification of the basis for grades to me on or before the first class meeting.

Date Submitted: ___ 1/11/2024 _____

SHERI MATTER AS THE DNP PROGRAM HEAD (02/07/2024)

Re: Email Access and Grade Adjudication

Oliver, Germine A <gobien5027@psu.edu>
Thu 2/8/2024 11:37 PM
To:Matter, Sheri <sxm1898@psu.edu>
Bcc:Michael Raffaele <michael@mykidslawyer.com>;bobadilo@centurylink.net <bobadilo@centurylink.net>

Dear Dr. Matter:

I received your message, below. I have emailed Dr. Wolgast to see if she will participate in the University Policy G-10 process. I will let you know if she does not. In addition, I have some questions about the leave of absence you recommend. I don't have any classes to register for this semester because I have completed all of my class requirements (or, more precisely, will have completed them when the incorrect grade and discrimination against me are rectified). All that is left to do is my defense. Do I understand correctly that Penn State will restore access to my email unless I take a leave of absence and thereby agree to postpone my defense, and my graduation, by at least a semester?

Thank you,
Germine

From: Matter, Sheri <sxm1898@psu.edu>
Sent: Wednesday, February 7, 2024 9:23 AM
To: Oliver, Germine A <gobien5027@psu.edu>; BOBADILA@CENTURYLINK.NET
<BOBADILA@CENTURYLINK.NET>
Cc: Matter, Sheri <sxm1898@psu.edu>
Subject: Email Access and Grade Adjudication

Good Afternoon Germine,

Per your request, the grade adjudication process will be implemented. According to University policy G-10, the process begins with the following steps:

1. A student who wishes to question or challenge the grade must first discuss grading practices and assignments with the instructor. It is expected that the student and instructor will try to eliminate any misunderstandings and will attempt to work out any disagreements over grades.

2. On the rare occasion that a student and instructor fail to resolve the grade dispute through informal means, the student should request grade mediation from the head of the academic program offering the course who will review the issue and take appropriate action to seek resolution.

Therefore, if you haven't already done so, your first task is to contact Dr. Kelly Wolgast to discuss the matter as stated above to see if the issue can be resolved. If there is no resolution, you will need to contact Dr Sheri Matter, the DNP Program Head, to request a review of your grade.

If the grade dispute is not resolved through the first two steps above, then Associate Dean Judith Hupcey will review your formal petition and seek any additional information she may need from you, the instructor, or others to determine if there is evidence that the instructor's assignment of the grade is in violation of Senate Policy 47-20. The Program Head will let Dean Badzek know whether the issue has been resolved through either of the steps above or if the formal petition needs to move to the next step of being reviewed by her. While your grade is being reviewed your termination from the program has been placed on hold.

We have also looked into the questions you had regarding access to your PSU email and other University systems. Although the College has not processed your termination in the system, we have learned that per University policy, if a student is not registered for courses in a given semester, it is flagged by the Registrar, which triggers the communications that you received regarding your email access, and the notation in LionPath indicating that you do not have an advisor assigned to you. In order for students to maintain access to their email during a semester in which they are not registered for courses, a *Leave of Absence* (LOA) request must be submitted by the student, so you will need to complete that process in order to maintain your program status during the grade adjudication process. Normally, all Leave of Absence (LOA) requests must be submitted to the Registrar's Office prior to the Friday before the first day of classes of the semester that the leave is being taken. Since that date has passed in this particular case, when you complete the form, please select fall 2024 for your LOA and we will change the semester to spring 2024 once the form comes through. Here is the hyperlink to request your LOA. https://www.registrar.psu.edu/enrollment/leaving/leave-absence.cfm.

For your reference, the procedures for a LOA are described in GSAD 900. If you have any questions regarding the actions that need to be taken as outlined above, please contact me so I can provide any additional information you need to move forward with both the adjudication and LOA processes.

Dr. Matter

Sheri Matter PhD, RN, NEA-BC
Assistant Dean for Graduate Professional Programs
Associate Teaching Professor
Ross and Carol Nese College of Nursing
Penn State University
311B Nursing Sciences Building
University Park, PA 16802-7000
Phone 717-582-6221
Zoom 312-446-1836
sxm1898@psu.edu

STUDENT COURSE HISTORY-COMPLETED AND PASSED ALL THE REQUIRED COURSES (1/24/2024)

Course History

101 rows

Class	Description	Term	Grade	Units	Status
NURS 596	Individual Studies	Fall 2023	F	2.00	✅ Taken >
NURS 834	D.N.P. Clin Pract	Spring 2023	A	3.00	✅ Taken >
NURS 835	D.N.P. Cap Proj	Spring 2023	B	2.00	✅ Taken >
NURS 835	D.N.P. Cap Proj	Fall 2022	B+	2.00	✅ Taken >
NURS 841	Eval in Nrsg Educ	Fall 2022	B	3.00	✅ Taken >
NURS 835	D.N.P. Cap Proj	Summer 2022	A-	2.00	✅ Taken >
NURS 834	D.N.P. Clin Pract	Spring 2022	A	2.00	✅ Taken >
NURS 837	EBP III	Spring 2022	A-	3.00	✅ Taken >
NURS 590	Colloquium	Fall 2021	A	1.00	✅ Taken >
NURS 830	EBP I	Fall 2021	A-	3.00	✅ Taken >
NURS 831	EBP II	Fall 2021	B	3.00	✅ Taken >
NURS 587	Rsch Ethics	Spring 2021	A	1.00	✅ Taken >
NURS 848A	Nurse Admin Practicum	Spring 2021	A	4.00	✅ Taken >
NURS 832	D.N.P. Leader I	Fall 2020	A	3.00	✅ Taken >
STAT 800	Applied Res Methds	Fall 2020	A	3.00	✅ Taken >
NURS 833	D.N.P. Leader II	Spring 2020	A-	3.00	✅ Taken >

AFFIRMATIVE ACTION OFFICE DECLINED TO INVESTIGATE THE COMPLAINT FOR THE FIRST TIME (02/01/2024)

From: Adair, Suzanne <sca917@psu.edu>
Sent: Thursday, February 1, 2024 6:33 PM
To: Oliver, Germine A <gobien5027@psu.edu>
Cc: Wright Watson, Denita Renee <Denita@psu.edu>
Subject: RE: OEOA 1/19/2024 meeting follow up

Hello Germine,

We have reviewed your email below and it is clear that you have significant concerns regarding the Office of Equal Opportunity and Access' (formerly the AAO) ability to conduct an impartial investigation of your discrimination complaint. Specifically, you indicated that "the involvement of the Office of Affirmative Action in communicating my dismissal raises questions about the impartiality of the process and the office's role in these decisions". Additionally, you noted your belief that "considering the complexity of the situation and the potential involvement of the Office of Affirmative Action in the processes leading to my dismissal, there is a clear need for an independent investigation". Given your stated mistrust of the University's ability to appropriately and objectively investigate your complaint, it appears that any investigation we conduct would not be viewed by you as fair or impartial. Therefore, we will not proceed with the internal investigation into your discrimination complaint and recommend that you submit your complaint to the Department of

Education's Office of Civil Rights (OCR), for an independent investigation per your request. Information for OCR can be found at the following website: https://www2.ed.gov/about/offices/list/ocr/index.html?src=mr.

Lastly, you have requested that your grade adjudication petition be moved forward to formally review the grade you received in the N596 independent study course. Your petition will be reviewed and the grade adjudication process will be implemented as requested.

Regards,
 Dr. Adair

Suzanne C. Adair, Ph.D.
Associate Vice President for Equal Opportunity and Access
328 Boucke Building
The Pennsylvania State University
University Park, PA 16802
(814) 863-0471

AFFIRMATIVE ACTION OFFICE DECLINED TO INVESTIGATE THE COMPLAINT A SECOND TIME (04/1/2024)

please direct me in the right direction, as the Office of the President directed me to your office for answers.

Thanks

From: Adair, Suzanne <sca917@psu.edu>
Sent: Monday, April 1, 2024 3:21 PM
To: Oliver, Germine A <gobien5027@psu.edu>
Cc: Pasko, Tetyana V <tvp2@psu.edu>
Subject: March 25th Complaint

Dear Germine,

We received the report you submitted to our office on March 25th, alleging discrimination, harassment and retaliation by the School of Nursing faculty and administration, as well as a number of other University employees, myself included. As I indicated in my February 1, 2024 email to you, given your clearly stated mistrust of the University's ability to appropriately and objectively investigate your complaint, we will not be proceeding with an internal investigation. I understand that in response to your March 22nd call to the Office of the President, you were directed to contact my office, which may have been what prompted your March 25th submission. However, in that February 1st email, I also recommended that given your stated feelings, you instead submit your complaint to the Department of Education's Office of Civil Rights (OCR) for an independent investigation per your earlier request. I am once again recommending that you submit your discrimination complaint directly to that agency. The information for OCR can be found at the following website: https://www2.ed.gov/about/offices/list/ocr/index.html?src=mr.

At this time, there is no need for continued outreach to various University offices regarding your discrimination complaint, as you have been provided with the information needed to report your concerns to OCR directly.

Regards,
Dr. Adair

Suzanne C. Adair, Ph.D.
Associate Vice President for Equal Opportunity and Access
328 Boucke Building
The Pennsylvania State University
University Park, PA 16802
(814) 863-0471
sca917@psu.edu

PDE CONTACT/VERBAL COMPLAINT
(01/04/2024)

Good afternoon,

Per our conversation, please find attached a Higher Education Complaint form for your spouse to complete and return, with relevant documentation, to my attention at ra-highereducation@pa.gov or to the following address:

> Pennsylvania Department of Education
> Division of Higher Education, Access, and Equity
> 607 South Drive, Floor 3E
> Harrisburg, PA 17020

Upon receipt of the complaint, this office will investigate potential violations of statute or regulations under its jurisdiction.

In addition, you can reach out the Pennsylvania Human Relations Commission regarding discrimination or bias in education: https://www.phrc.pa.gov/Complaints/Pages/How-to-File-a-Complaint.aspx

Please feel free to contact me with any questions.

Kind regards,

Michelle Simmons | Administrative Assistant
she/her/hers
Department of Education | Division of Higher Education, Access, and Equity
Phone: 717.783.6786 | www.education.pa.gov

From: +1 717-361-1655 <+17173611655>
Sent: Thursday, January 4, 2024 12:43 PM
To: Simmons, Michelle <michellsim@pa.gov>
Subject: [External] Voice Mail (1 minute and 10 seconds)

ATTENTION: *This email message is from an external sender. Do not open links or attachments from unknown senders. To report suspicious email, use the Report Phishing button in Outlook.*

Yes, Hello, Good afternoon. My name is Benjamin Johnson. My phone number is 717, 3611655. I am calling in regards to a situation at Penn State University at the College of Nursing. It is a situation of discrimination, harassment and retaliation it seems, and we need help. At least we need to be able to lodge a complaint. We don't know what to do. Please give me a call, at least let me know. Help me understand. Please help me find a way forward. This is a very distressful situation for my family and I am seeking help any way I can at this point. Again, my name is Benjamin Johnson. This situation is at Penn State University. The nursing program, the nursing school. My number is 717, 361-1655. Thank you.

PHRC CONTACT/VERBAL COMPLAINT (01/25/2024)

Good morning,
Attached is an Employment and Education Accommodation Intake form for your complaint.
Intake Scheduling will contact you in order to schedule an appointment, in order to draft a complaint.
Please email the completed form to phrc@pa.gov.
Thank you for contacting the PHRC.
Pennsylvania Human Relation Commission
333 Market Street, 8th Floor | Harrisburg PA 17101-2210
Phone: 717-787-4410 | Fax: 717-787-0420
www.phrc.pa.gov

Discrimination is illegal in PA. Get the facts at www.phrc.pa.gov.
The information transmitted is intended only for the person or entity to whom it is addressed and may contain confidential and/or privileged material. Any use of this information other than by the intended recipient is prohibited. If you receive this message in error, please send a reply e-mail to the sender and delete the material from any and all computers. Unintended transmissions shall not constitute waiver of the attorney-client or any other privilege.

OFFICE FOR CIVIL RIGHTS (OCR) DISMISSAL LETTER (08/13/2024)

In your call with OCR staff on June 6, 2024, you stated that you also filed the same allegations in your OCR complaint with the Pennsylvania Human Rights Commission (PHRC). You subsequently provided OCR with a copy of your PHRC complaint and the University's response. OCR reviewed the PHRC complaint and had determined that you raised the same allegations with PHRC that you are raising with OCR. In addition, OCR has confirmed that the PHRC is proceeding with its investigation of that complaint.

OCR anticipates that PHRC will investigate these allegations, the remedies obtained will be the same as those that would be obtained if OCR were to find a violation regarding the allegations, and there will be a comparable resolution process under comparable legal standards. Consequently, OCR is dismissing your complaint pursuant to Section 110(a)(1) of the CPM, effective the date of this letter.

You may refile your complaint within 60 days of the completion of PHRC's processing of your complaint. Generally, OCR will not conduct its own investigation but instead, will review the results of the other entity's determination and decide whether the other entity provided a comparable resolution process in which it applied comparable legal standards.

We did not notify the University of your complaint. Nevertheless, please be advised that the University must not harass, coerce, intimidate, discriminate, or otherwise retaliate against an individual because that individual asserts a right or privilege under a law enforced by OCR or files a complaint, testifies, assists, or participates in a proceeding under a law enforced by OCR. If this happens, the individual may file a retaliation complaint with OCR.

Under the Freedom of Information Act, it may be necessary to release this document and related correspondence and records upon request. If OCR receives such a request, it will seek to protect, to the extent provided by law, personally identifiable information, that, if released, could reasonably be expected to constitute an unwarranted invasion of personal privacy.

If you have any questions about this letter, you may contact Bradley Moore, the OCR attorney assigned to this complaint, at (215) 656-8502 or Bradley.Moore@ed.gov.

Sincerely,

CHAD DION LASSITER/PHRC CONFLICT OF INTEREST- UNIVERSITY BANQUET (02/26/2024)

MLK Banquet Scholarship Effort

2024 Honorees and Keynote Speaker

2023 Honorees

Theme: Where Do We Go From Here: Chaos or Community?

Keynote Speaker

CHAD DION LASSITER

Chad Dion Lassiter is a national expert in the field of American race relations. He has worked on race, peace, and poverty-related issues in the United States, Africa, Canada, Haiti, Israel, and Norway, and is called upon frequently by media outlets to provide commentary on race relations and potential solutions. In April 2023, Lassiter was appointed by President Biden to the Presidential Advisory Commission on Advancing Educational Equity, Excellence, and Economic Opportunities for Black Americans.

Lassiter is the current Executive Director of the Pennsylvania Human Relations Commission, where, over his five years in this position, he has continued to push the Commonwealth forward in the spaces of DEI training, unconscious bias training, and anti-racism training. He developed and launched a "No Hate in Our State Townhall" to address the surge of white nationalism in Pennsylvania, as well as a "Social Justice Lecture Series" to provide an outlet for the communities in the Commonwealth to discuss imperative issues and serve as a Racial Reduction Response team for those communities impacted by hatred. He oversees a staff of 87 with three regional offices that serve the 67 counties in Pennsylvania and manages an annual budget of $11 million dollars.

During his appointment, Lassiter has also developed programs such as a "Global Social Justice Initiative," "Black and Jewish Beloved Community Dialogue," and the "College Race Dialogue Initiative."

Chad Dion Lassiter, MSW
Executive Director
Pennsylvania Human Relations Commission

1:05 / 2:13

2024 Dr. Martin Luther King, Jr. Commemorative Banquet Theme: Where...

PennState
Harrisburg

REPORT A CONCERN | VISIT | APPLY | GIVE
Academics + | Admissions and Financial Aid + | Research | Information For +

MLK Banquet Scholarship Effort

2024 Honorees and Keynote Speaker

2023 Honorees

Theme: Where Do We Go From Here: Chaos or Community?

Keynote Speaker

CHAD DION LASSITER

Chad Dion Lassiter is a national expert in the field of American race relations. He has worked on race, peace, and poverty-related issues in the United States, Africa, Canada, Haiti, Israel, and Norway, and is called upon frequently by media outlets to provide commentary on race relations and potential solutions. In April 2023, Lassiter was appointed by President Biden to the Presidential Advisory Commission on Advancing Educational Equity, Excellence, and Economic Opportunities for Black Americans.

Lassiter is the current Executive Director of the Pennsylvania Human Relations Commission, where, over his five years in this position, he has continued to push the Commonwealth forward in the spaces of DEI training, unconscious bias training, and anti-racism training. He developed and launched a "No Hate in Our State Townhall" to address the surge of white nationalism in Pennsylvania, as well as a "Social Justice Lecture Series" to provide an outlet for the communities in the Commonwealth to discuss imperative issues and serve as a Racial Reduction Response team for those communities impacted by hatred. He oversees a staff of 87 with three regional offices that serve the 67 counties in Pennsylvania and manages an annual budget of $11 million dollars.

During his appointment, Lassiter has also developed programs such as a "Global Social Justice Initiative," "Black and Jewish Beloved Community Dialogue," and the "College Race Dialogue Initiative."

Chad Dion Lassiter, MSW
Executive Director
Pennsylvania Human Relations Commission

1:05 / 2:13

2024 Dr. Martin Luther King, Jr. Commemorative Banquet Theme: Where...

7 · 103 views

Like   Comment   Share

Penn State Harrisburg
February 26, 2024

Follow

Overview   Comments

As we continue to celebrate Black History Month, we take a look back at the college's Martin Luther King Commemorative Banquet. The event, themed "Where Do We Go From Here: Chaos or Community?", included dinner and entertainment and recognized commun...
See more

Be the first to leave a comment.

Comment as

Explore more in Video

Home   Live

PHRC CONFLICT OF INTEREST DISMISSAL LETTER (11/06/2024)

pennsylvania
HUMAN RELATIONS COMMISSION

November 6, 2024

Germine Oliver
667 Mount Gretna Road
Elizabethtown, PA 17022

Andrew T Simmons
50 S 16TH ST
STE 3200
Philadelphia, PA 19102

RE: Germine Oliver vs. Penn State Ross and Carol Nese College of Nursing
   PHRC Case No. 202317185

Dear Parties:

The Pennsylvania Human Relations Commission reviewed the above-referenced Complaint and considers this case closed on the date of this letter because:

There was insufficient evidence to establish discrimination and a copy of this finding is enclosed.

The Pennsylvania Human Relations Act affords both the Complainant and the Respondent the opportunity to comment after the final disposition of the Complaint. Written comments may be submitted to the Director of Enforcement, 333 Market Street, 8th Floor, Harrisburg, PA 17101. In addition, enclosed is a Notice of Complainant's Rights that explains the right and process to appeal closure by filing a Request for Preliminary Hearing or a Complaint* in the Court of Common Pleas pursuant to 43 P.S. Section 962(c). *Please note that the Complaint must be filed within two years of the date of this closure notice.

Sincerely:

Chad Dion Lassiter, MSW

Chad Dion Lassiter, MSW
Executive Director

cc:

PHRC CONFLICT OF INTEREST DISMISSAL LETTER/COPY-PASTE DECISION (07/25/2025)

pennsylvania
HUMAN RELATIONS COMMISSION

July 25, 2025

Germine Oliver
PO Box 214
Middletown, PA 17057

Andrew T Simmons
Two Liberty Place
50 S. 16th Street Suite 3200
Philadelphia, PA 19102

RE: Germine Oliver vs. Penn State Ross and Carol Nese College of Nursing
    PHRC Case No. 202317185

Dear Parties:

The Pennsylvania Human Relations Commission reviewed the above-referenced Complaint and considers this case closed on the date of this letter because:

There was insufficient evidence to establish discrimination and a copy of this finding is enclosed.

The Pennsylvania Human Relations Act affords both the Complainant and the Respondent the opportunity to comment after the final disposition of the Complaint. Written comments may be submitted to the Director of Enforcement, 333 Market Street, 8th Floor, Harrisburg, PA 17101. In addition, enclosed is a Notice of Complainant's Rights that explains the right and process to appeal closure by filing a Request for Preliminary Hearing or a Complaint* in the Court of Common Pleas pursuant to 43 P.S. Section 962(c). *Please note that the Complaint must be filed within two years of the date of this closure notice.

Sincerely:

Chad Dion Lassiter MSW

Chad Dion Lassiter, MSW
Executive Director

cc:

INDIVIDUALS NAMED IN THE
INITIAL COMPLAINT INCLUDE
ASSOCIATE DEAN JUDITH HUPCEY
(01/02/2024)

Who do you believe is responsible for the alleged discrimination, harassment or retaliatory act/behavior? (Please provide names and job titles of all individuals involved
I believe the following individuals, along with their respective job titles, are responsible for the alleged discrimination, harassment, or retaliatory behavior:

Sheri Matter (Project Chair/Advisor/Dean). The primary individual responsible is my project chair, who also served as my advisor in the DNP program and holds the position of dean at the School of Nursing. This individual's unsupportive behavior and significant role in denying me the opportunity to present my final project suggest her central involvement in the discriminatory and retaliatory actions.

Kelly Gallagher (Course Instructor). The instructor of the course (Nursing 835) in which I received a zero grade played a key role in what I perceive as retaliatory and discriminatory actions. Her direct involvement in grading and subsequent negative remarks towards me indicates her responsibility for these matters.

Workplace Colleagues (Staff members). Several colleagues at my workplace connected with the university, engaged in harassing behavior. They mocked my academic progress in the DNP program and my accent, contributing to a hostile work environment.

Judith Hupcey (Dean). Dean Judith Hupcey, responsible for grade adjudication, initially dismissed my claim under a false pretext and later changed my grade after I provided the supporting documents. However, she also dismissed my request for a new committee and made several disparaging remarks, which led me to believe her desire to retaliate against me in the light of having to change her initial decisions, also as an attempt to protect Dean Sheri Matter. Her actions and decisions significantly affected my academic standing and contributed to the overall situation.

Kelly Wolgast (New Project Chair) and Committee Members (Susan Leight, Sheldon Fields). The new project chair assigned by Dean Judith Hupcey, along with the two committee members, were involved in the later stages of my academic journey. Their actions, including questioning the integrity of my project and suggesting that I redo the entire project under unrealistic time constraints, were part of the retaliatory behavior I experienced.

Cara Exten and Rachel Alyson (Committee Members). These individuals were part of my previous committee. They provided no feedback on the initial project.

Tabitha Oman (University Ethics Department) and Stephanie Preston (University Equity Department). While their involvement was initially in response to my husband's request for mediation, the ethics department's actions indirectly influenced the unfolding events, especially concerning the enrollment in the independent course for project completion.

Each of these individuals, through their actions, omissions, and decisions within their professional capacities at the university and the School of Nursing, contributed to the experiences I perceive as discriminatory, harassing, and retaliatory. Their collective influence significantly impacted my academic experience and progression within the DNP program.

UNIVERSITY PRESIDENT BENDAPUDI CLOSED THE MATTER IN VIOLATION OF POLICY GCAC-803 (04/19/2024)

Mr. Johnson,

As Senior Vice President and Chief of Staff, I help President Bendapudi respond to emails and important issues. Thank you for your email. We have been informed that the Grade Adjudication process has been concluded with the Dean's review and decision, which is final. Additionally, we understand that the Office of Equal Opportunity and Access (formerly the Affirmative Action Office) has directed you to contact the Department of Education's Office of Civil Rights with any further concerns, and that you have filed a complaint with the Pennsylvania Department of Education, which the University will respond to as required. Based on this information, there will be no further action taken and the matter is considered closed.

Sincerely,

Michael Wade Smith
Senior Vice President and Chief of Staff

ANNOTATED POLICY GCAC-803
(BEFORE SCHOOL MODIFICATION
IN JULY 2024)

Home / Graduate Education Policies / GCAC-803

◉ **Purpose**

To describe the procedure by which a graduate student is terminated from a graduate program for unsatisfactory scholarship.

⟨⟩ **Scope**

All graduate students.

Background ⌄

Policy Statement

1. Where the basis for unsatisfactory scholarship is behavior that is believed to fall within the Code of Conduct, it should first be referred to the Office of Student Conduct for adjudication. (See GCAC-801 Conduct).

    a. If the Office of Student Conduct determines that the graduate student did not engage in a Code of Conduct behavior, and if the sole basis for unsatisfactory scholarship was if the behavior did fall within the Code of Conduct, no further action should be taken.

    b. If the Office of Student Conduct determines the graduate student has engaged in a Code of Conduct behavior and issues a sanction(s), this does constitute unsatisfactory scholarship and further action may be taken by the program and/or the Graduate School.

2. When a graduate program head, program committee, or, in the case of a doctoral student, the doctoral committee determines that the program of a graduate student must be terminated for unsatisfactory scholarship, the student must be given advance notice, in writing, which in general terms shall advise the student of the reasons for the termination.

    a. Examples of unsatisfactory scholarship may include, but are not limited to:

        i. failure to exhibit and promote the highest ethical, moral, and professional standards;

        ii. inadequate grade-point average;

        iii. failure to obtain satisfactory grades in required courses for the program;

        iv. failure to make satisfactory progress in research or other activities related to the culminating experience; or

        v. failing the qualifying, comprehensive, or final oral examination for doctoral students.

3. Upon receipt of this notice, the student has the opportunity to seek a review of the decision. If the student desires such a review, the student must, within ten days of receipt of the notice, submit a written appeal to the program head.

4. If the student alleges that discrimination either was the reason for the termination or caused the unsatisfactory scholarship, and the discrimination or harassment was committed by an individual in a role of authority, such as an administrator, faculty member, instructor, teaching assistant, or research assistant, the matter shall be referred to the Affirmative Action Office of the University, established to review such claims.

   a. If the Affirmative Action Office determines that the student's allegation has merit, the Affirmative Action Office will manage the investigation and report back to the program head and any other University office as appropriate.

   b. If the Affirmative Action Office determines that the student's allegation is unfounded, the graduate program head then provides an opportunity for the student to meet with him/her and, if applicable, the program committee, doctoral committee, or other faculty involved in the decision to terminate the student's program.

5. If there is no allegation of discrimination within the written appeal, then the graduate program head provides an opportunity for the student to meet with the faculty member(s) who made the decision to terminate the student's program.

   a. This meeting must be held within 30 days of receipt of the student's written appeal.

      i. Under extraordinary circumstances, either party may request a stay to the 30-day time limit. A request for such a stay must include a justification and indicate the desired duration of the stay, and be directed to the Dean of the Graduate School, whose decision on the stay will be final.

   b. Formal rules of evidence are not applicable to the meeting, and attorneys are not permitted to represent any person attending the meeting.

   c. If the student's faculty adviser would not otherwise be present (i.e., was not involved in the decision to terminate), the adviser should be permitted to attend this meeting if requested by the student or graduate program head, or if the adviser wishes to do so.

   d. The graduate program head is responsible for ensuring that minutes of the meeting are taken and copies distributed to all those in attendance.

6. Following this meeting, the graduate program head must notify the student within five days, in writing, whether the termination decision has been sustained or reversed.

   a. If it is sustained, the graduate program head shall notify the Dean of the Graduate School. If the termination is based upon failure to exhibit and promote the highest ethical, moral, and professional standards expected of graduate students, the Graduate School may also make a determination to dismiss the student from continued or future enrollment in any graduate program at the University. If the Graduate School dismisses the student from continued or future enrollment in any graduate program at the University, notification of that decision will be given to the student within this time frame as well.

7. Within five days of receiving this notice of termination for unsatisfactory scholarship, the student may make a written request to the Dean of the Graduate School for a further review of the decision. The student is permitted to submit additional information or statements in writing.

   a. Although not required to do so, the Dean of the Graduate School may meet with the student and/or graduate program head, or request additional information from the student and/or graduate program head. If a meeting is held, the student may not be represented by an attorney, but may have present a faculty adviser of his or her choice.

University, notification of that decision will be given to the student within this time frame as well.

7. Within five days of receiving this notice of termination for unsatisfactory scholarship, the student may make a written request to the Dean of the Graduate School for a further review of the decision. The student is permitted to submit additional information or statements in writing.

   a. Although not required to do so, the Dean of the Graduate School may meet with the student and/or graduate program head, or request additional information from the student and/or the graduate program head. If a meeting is held, the student may not be represented by an attorney, but may have present a faculty adviser of his or her choice.

   b. The standard of review by the Graduate School is whether the decision to terminate for unsatisfactory scholarship was arbitrary and capricious. The terms "arbitrary and capricious" mean that the decision to terminate is not supportable on any rational basis, or that there is no evidence upon which the decision may be based. The Graduate School does not review faculty judgments as to the quality of a student's academic performance (e.g., the quality of a thesis or dissertation, performance on a comprehensive examination, etc.), but only whether a program's decision was arbitrary and capricious, including in cases of failure to exhibit and promote the highest ethical, moral, and professional standards expected of graduate students.

8. After this review, the Dean of the Graduate School either sustains the termination or, if he/she determines that the decision was arbitrary and capricious, reverses the decision with any corrective action, and permits the student to continue in the program.

   a. If the termination is sustained, the Dean of the Graduate School directs, at their discretion for termination from the Graduate School and, at the discretion of the program for termination from only the graduate program in which the student is enrolled, that the termination be entered on the student's transcript.

   b. The Dean of the Graduate School gives written notice of the decision to the program head and to the student within three weeks of receipt of the student's written request to the Dean.

   c. In the event of a reversal, such written notice shall contain a statement of the basis upon which the decision was made.

9. The decision by the Dean of the Graduate School is final.

10. A registration hold may be placed on the student's records while action is pending under these procedures.

11. Nothing in this policy is intended to constitute a contract or contractual terms. No provisions of this policy shall confer contractual rights upon any parties. To the extent that this policy may be applicable to faculty or staff, the terms outlined herein do not constitute terms, benefits, or conditions of employment. The terms set forth herein are subject to change unilaterally and without notice by University administration.

Revision History

- Adapted from the Graduate Bulletin: June 2018.
- Revisions proposed by the Graduate Council Committee on Academic Standards and approved by Graduate Council, February 2013.
- Revisions by the Graduate Council Committee on Academic Standards, January 2008.
- Revised by special Ad Hoc Committee on Student-Related Policies, April 2007.
- Revised by special Ad Hoc Committee on Student-Related Policies, August 2005
- Approved by the Graduate Council, May 8, 2002.
  - New policy.

ATTORNEYS HAVE A DUTY OF CANDOR (THEIR STATEMENT ON 07/15/2024 IS DEMONSTRABLY FALSE)

DUE PROCESS VIOLATIONS

FALSE STATEMENT TO A TRIBUNAL

11. Denied as stated. On February 7, 2024, Respondent informed Complainant that it would conduct a grade adjudication, despite the fact that Complainant had not requested a grade adjudication prior to her January 31, 2024, academic dismissal letter from the College of Nursing. By way of further response, Respondent informed Complainant that, pursuant to Penn State policy, she could request a Leave of Absence in order to maintain access to her Penn State email account and other amenities because Complainant had not registered for any classes for the Spring 2024 semester at that time.

Respectfully submitted,

BUCHANAN INGERSOLL & ROONEY PC

PROFESSIONAL MISCONDUCT BY THE ATTORNEYS

/s/ George C. Morrison
George C. Morrison, Esq. (PA 203223)
Keith M. Lee, Esq. (PA 330237)
Andrew T. Simmons, Esq. (PA 331973)
Two Liberty Place
50 S. 16th Street, Suite 3200
Philadelphia, PA 19102
(215) 665-3909

Dated: July 15, 2024   *Counsel for Respondent*

Request made on January 24, 2024

DUE PROCESS VIOLATIONS EVIDENCE

From: Oliver, Germine <obien5027@psu.edu>
Sent: Wednesday, January 24, 2024 3:28 PM
To: Hupcey, Judith E <jhupcey@psu.edu>; Badzek, Laurie <lzb340@psu.edu>; Matter, Sheri <sxm1898@psu.edu>; Wright Watson, Denita Renee <Denita@psu.edu>; Adair, Suzanne <sca917@psu.edu>; Fong, Duncan King-Hoi <i2v@psu.edu>; Grad Dean's Office <graddeansoffice@psu.edu>; Oman, Tabitha <txo5152@psu.edu>
Subject: Grade Adjudication request

Hello,

To whom it may concern.

Below is my formal request for a grade adjudication in the N596 independent study (Fall 2023).

The grade received violates school policy 47-20. The instructor did not provide a written (paper or electronic form) notification of the basis for grades to me on or before the first class meeting.

Also, I have been informed in an email correspondence by a representative from the office of Affirmative Action that I am being terminated from the nursing program for missing previously specified deadlines. This is another excuse to justify a blatant discriminatory act against my person at Penn State University. I intend to challenge these unsubstantiated claims as vigorously as Penn State policy guidelines would allow. It is my understanding that there are no such stipulations neither in school policy nor in the student handbook for the DNP program. I completed all the benchmarks and other requirements, as specified in the DNP program and within the prescribed timeline, except for the oral presentation, which is beyond my purview.

I intend to appeal any arbitrary decisions if and when they are communicated to me officially.

Please see attached document for the grade adjudication.

Germine Oliver

CONFLICT OF INTEREST BY FRANK
MILLER AT THE FEDERAL LEVEL
(SPPO) TO PROTECT PENN STATE

Jul 2014 - Jan 2019 · 4 yrs 7 mos

US Department of Education
2 yrs 7 mos

Management and Program Analyst
Aug 2013 - Jun 2014 · 11 mos

Education Program Specialist
Dec 2011 - Aug 2013 · 1 yr 9 mos

Division Chief, Western Operations and Program Monitoring
PA Department of Education
Apr 2007 - Dec 2011 · 4 yrs 9 mos

Human Services Program Supervisor
PA Department of Public Welfare
Oct 2005 - Apr 2006 · 7 mos
Greater Harrisburg Area

Drug and Alcohol Licensing Specialist Supervisor
PA Department of Health
Dec 1999 - Oct 2005 · 5 yrs 11 mos
Greater Harrisburg Area

Education

University of Phoenix
Master of Science (M.S.), Computer Information Systems
2004 - 2006

Penn State University
Bachelor of Science (B.S.), Health Policy and Administration
1988 - 1993

CONFLICT OF INTEREST BY CHAD
DION LASSITER HONORED BY PENN
STATE AT BANQUET AND KEYNOTE
SPEECH-AT THE STATE LEVEL
(PHRC) PROTECT PENN STATE 1

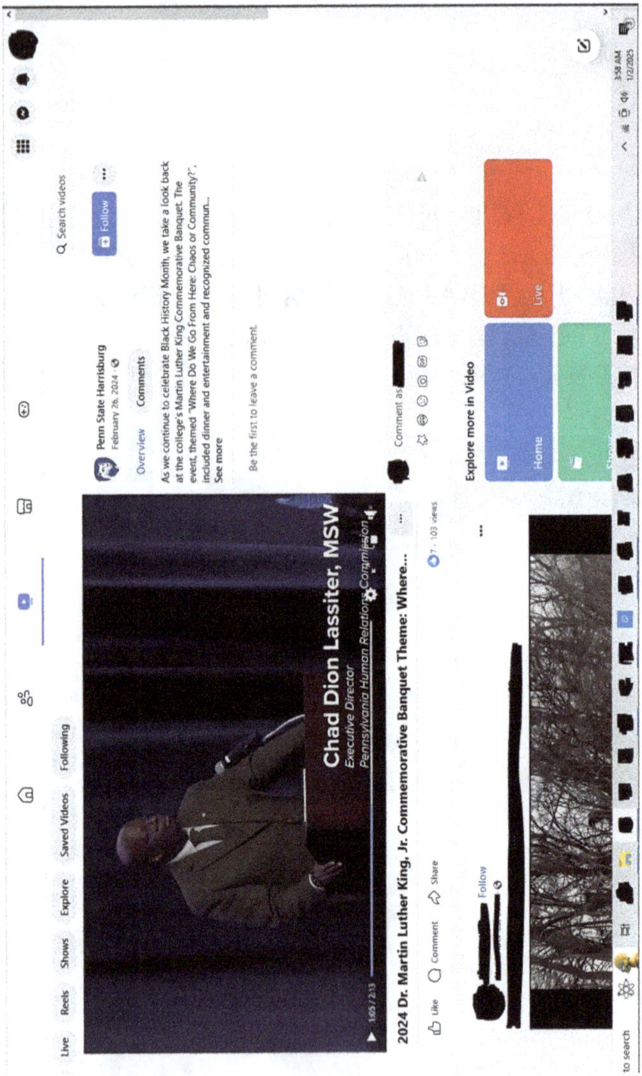

CONFLICT OF INTEREST-CHAD
DION LASSITER HONORED BY PENN
STATE-AT THE STATE LEVEL (PHRC)
PROTECT PENN STATE 2

Theme: Where Do We Go From Here: Chaos or Community?

Keynote Speaker

CHAD DION LASSITER

Chad Dion Lassiter is a national expert in the field of American race relations. He has worked on race, peace, and poverty-related issues in the United States, Africa, Canada, Haiti, Israel, and Norway, and is called upon frequently by media outlets to provide commentary on race relations and potential solutions. In April 2023, Lassiter was appointed by President Biden to the Presidential Advisory Commission on Advancing Educational Equity, Excellence, and Economic Opportunities for Black Americans.

Lassiter is the current Executive Director of the Pennsylvania Human Relations Commission, where, over his five years in this position, he has continued to push the Commonwealth forward in the spaces of DEI training, unconscious bias training, and anti-racism training. He developed and launched a "No Hate in Our State Townhall" to address the surge of white nationalism in Pennsylvania, as well as a "Social Justice Lecture Series" to provide an outlet for the communities in the Commonwealth to discuss imperative issues and serve as a Racial Reduction Response team for those communities impacted by hatred. He oversees a staff of 87 with three regional offices that serve the 67 counties in Pennsylvania and manages an annual budget of $11 million dollars.

During his appointment, Lassiter has also developed programs such as a "Global Social Justice Initiative," "Black and Jewish Beloved Community Dialogue," and the "College Race Dialogue Initiative."

PHRC LIED ABOUT STUDENT
RECORD TO PROTECT PENN STATE

Proof 8: PHRC made demonstrably false statements about my academic records

    1. Disenrollment Due to Retaliation (Opposed Unlawful Activity)

In order to prevail in a case alleging disenrollment due to retaliation, Complainant must show that there is a causal connection between her protected activity and the adverse action taken by Respondent. The evidence shows that on January 2, 2024, Complainant filed a discrimination complaint with Respondent alleging disparate treatment due to her age, race, color, national origin, sex, gender, and marital/family status. The evidence shows that in January 2023, Respondent notified Complainant of several issues with her paper/project. The evidence shows that Complainant acknowledged the issues stating that she believed the paper/project could be fixed and requested guidance on how to proceed. The evidence shows that Respondent provided a timeline for Complainant with benchmarks from February 2023 through April 2023, May 2023 through June 2023, and her anticipated project and final paper completion on August 1, 2023. The evidence shows that as of May 2023, Complainant received two grades below a B which would cause her dismissal from the program. The evidence shows that Respondent permitted Complainant to remain in the program provided she received a B or better in all subsequent courses. The evidence shows that on December 4, 2023, Respondent informed Complainant that her project was not approved. The evidence shows that on December 6, 2023, Complainant agreed to revise her project due to continuing issues but stopped communicating with her advisor. The evidence shows that on January 31, 2024, Respondent dismissed Complainant from its Doctor of Nurse Practitioner program due to her unsuccessful completion of requirements. The evidence shows that Respondent's decision was upheld on April 8, 2024, following the grade adjudication process. The evidence supports that Respondent communicated deficiencies in Complainant's work and performance well before her complaint.

As such, the investigation is unable to establish a causal connection between Complainant's protected activity and her dismissal.

Therefore, PHRC concludes that there is insufficient evidence to support a finding of probable cause that Penn State Ross and Carol Nese College of Nursing violated the Pennsylvania Human Relations Act.

/s/ Meghan E. Weisen

Investigator

Date: October 23, 2024

COURSE HISTORY PROVES THAT PHRC MADE FALSE STATEMENT ABOUT STUDENT RECORD TO PROTECT PENN STATE

Proof 9: Refute PHRC's false statements about my academic records

Course History

101 rows

Class	Description	Term	Grade	Units	Status
NURS 596	Individual Studies	Fall 2023	F	2.00	✓ Taken	>
NURS 834	D.N.P. Clin Pract	Spring 2023	A	3.00	✓ Taken	>
NURS 835	D.N.P. Cap Proj	Spring 2023	B	2.00	✓ Taken	>
NURS 835	D.N.P. Cap Proj	Fall 2022	B+	2.00	✓ Taken	>
NURS 841	Eval in Nrsg Educ	Fall 2022	B	3.00	✓ Taken	>
NURS 835	D.N.P. Cap Proj	Summer 2022	A-	2.00	✓ Taken	>
NURS 834	D.N.P. Clin Pract	Spring 2022	A	2.00	✓ Taken	>
NURS 837	EBP III	Spring 2022	A-	3.00	✓ Taken	>
NURS 590	Colloquium	Fall 2021	A	1.00	✓ Taken	>
NURS 830	EBP I	Fall 2021	A-	3.00	✓ Taken	>
NURS 831	EBP II	Fall 2021	B	3.00	✓ Taken	>
NURS 587	Rsch Ethics	Spring 2021	A	1.00	✓ Taken	>
NURS 848A	Nurse Admin Practicum	Spring 2021	A	4.00	✓ Taken	>
NURS 832	D.N.P. Leader I	Fall 2020	A	3.00	✓ Taken	>
STAT 800	Applied Res Methds	Fall 2020	A	3.00	✓ Taken	>
NURS 833	D.N.P. Leader II	Spring 2020	A-	3.00	✓ Taken	>

of 2

1/24/2024, 8:15 PM

EVIDENCE THAT PENN STATE UNIVERSITY LIED ABOUT STUDENT ACADEMIC RECORD

Proof 10: As of June 7, 2023, I did not have any remaining required course in the DNP program

Please meet with your committee to develop your scholarly project moving forward.

Germine, I will not respond to any additional emails from you. This decision is final, and if you continue to make unfounded accusations against your committee members, it will be hard for us to reconstitute another committee. We know that you have checked all the course boxes for the DNP degree; however, the DNP project is not just a check box; this is a doctoral project. You need to complete a scholarly project and paper before we confer you a doctoral degree.

We all want you to be successful. But this requires you to work with your committee and submit doctoral-level work. Moving forward, you will need to register for a 2-3 credit independent study each semester until you are approved to do your final presentation and your final paper is accepted. Please work with Dr. Wolgast on these independent studies.

Regards,

Dr. Hupcey

....

Judith E. Hupcey, Ed.D., CRNP, FAAN
Professor of Nursing & Medicine
Associate Dean for Research & Innovation
Interim Associate Dean for Graduate Education
Ross and Carol Nese
College of Nursing
The Pennsylvania State University

PHRC REOPENED CASE ON FEBRUARY 2025 TO PROTECT PENN STATE

pennsylvania
HUMAN RELATIONS COMMISSION

February 20, 2025

Germine Oliver
667 Mount Gretna Road
Elizabethtown, PA 17022

Andrew T Simmons
Two Liberty Place
50 S. 16th Street
Suite 3200
Philadelphia, PA 19102

RE: Germine Oliver vs. Penn State Ross and Carol Nese College of Nursing
      PHRC Case No. 202317185
      EEOC Case No.   N/A

Dear Parties,

This correspondence is to notify you that the Pennsylvania Human Relations
Commission has reopened the above-referenced case for further investigation. The case
is being referred to the Commission's Harrisburg Regional Office.

PHRC staff will be in contact with you regarding this case.

Sincerely,

Enforcement Division
PA Human Relations Commission

cc:

PHRC DELIVERED COPY-PASTE DECISION TO PROTECT PENN STATE NOVEMBER 6, 2024 AND JULY 25, 2025

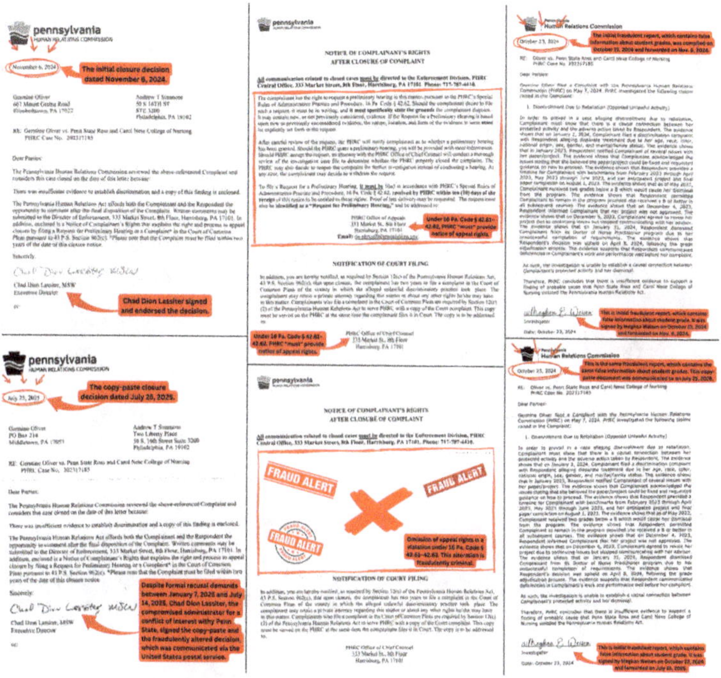
pennsylvania
HUMAN RELATIONS COMMISSION
November 6, 2024
The initial closure decision dated November 6, 2024.
Chad Dion Lassiter, MSW
Executive Director
Chad Dion Lassiter signed and endorsed the decision.
pennsylvania
HUMAN RELATIONS COMMISSION
July 25, 2025
The copy-paste closure decision dated July 25, 2025.
Despite formal recusal demands between January 7, 2025 and July 14, 2025, Chad Dion Lassiter, the compromised administrator for a conflict of interest withy Penn State, signed the copy-paste and the fraudulently altered decision, which was communicated via the United States postal service.
NOTICE OF COMPLAINANT'S RIGHTS
AFTER CLOSURE OF COMPLAINT
Under 16 Pa. Code § 42.61–42.62, PHRC "must" provide notice of appeal rights.
NOTIFICATION OF COURT FILING
Under 16 Pa. Code § 42.61–42.62, PHRC "must" provide notice of appeal rights.
NOTICE OF COMPLAINANT'S RIGHTS
AFTER CLOSURE OF COMPLAINT
FRAUD ALERT
FRAUD ALERT
FRAUD ALERT
Omission of appeal rights is a violation under 16 Pa. Code § 42.61–42.62. This alteration is fraudulently criminal.
NOTIFICATION OF COURT FILING
Human Relations Commission
October 23, 2024
The initial fraudulent report, which contains false information about student grades, was compiled on October 23, 2024 and forwarded on Nov. 6, 2024.
Human Relations Commission
October 23, 2024
This is the same fraudulent report, which contains the same false information about student grades. This copy-paste document was communicated to us July 25, 2025.

BUCHANAN INGERSOLL & ROONEY
PC -PROFESSIONAL MISCONDUCT
AND LIES TO PROTECT PENN STATE
JULY 15 2025

DUE PROCESS VIOLATIONS **FALSE STATEMENT TO A TRIBUNAL**

11. Denied as stated. On February 7, 2024, Respondent informed Complainant that it would conduct a grade adjudication, despite the fact that Complainant had not requested a grade adjudication prior to her January 31, 2024 academic dismissal letter from the College of Nursing. By way of further response, Respondent informed Complainant that, pursuant to Penn State policy, she could request a Leave of Absence in order to maintain access to her Penn State email account and other amenities because Complainant had not registered for any classes for the Spring 2024 semester at that time.

Respectfully submitted,

BUCHANAN INGERSOLL & ROONEY PC

/s/ George C. Morrison
George C. Morrison, Esq. (PA 203223)
Keith M. Lee, Esq. (PA 330237)
Andrew T. Simmons, Esq. (PA 331973)
Two Liberty Place
50 S. 16th Street, Suite 3200
Philadelphia, PA 19102
(215) 665-3900

PROFESSIONAL MISCONDUCT BY THE ATTORNEYS

Dated: July 15, 2024   Counsel for Respondent

From: Adair, Suzanne <sla917@psu.edu>
Sent: Thursday, February 1, 2024 6:33 PM
To: Oliver, Germine A <gobien502@psu.edu>
Cc: Wright Watson, Denita Renee <Denita@psu.edu>
Subject: RE: OEOA 1/18/2024 meeting follow up

University responded to January 24, 2024 request on February 1, 2024

Hello Germine,

We have reviewed your email below and it is clear that you have significant concerns regarding the Office of Equal Opportunity and Access (formerly the AAO) ability to conduct an impartial investigation of your discrimination complaint. Specifically, you indicated that "the involvement of the Office of Affirmative Action in communicating my dismissal raises questions about the impartiality of the process and the office's role in these decisions". Additionally, you noted your belief that "considering the complexity of the situation and the potential involvement of the Office of Affirmative Action in the processes leading to my dismissal, there is a clear need for an independent investigation". Given your stated mistrust of the University's ability to appropriately and objectively investigate your complaint, it appears that any investigation we conduct would not be viewed by you as fair or impartial. Therefore, we will not proceed with the internal investigation into your discrimination complaint and recommend that you submit your complaint to the Department of

3/28/2024, 11

https://outlook.office.com/mail/id/AAQkAOQEMmUzNjg3LTI

Education's Office of Civil Rights (OCR), for an independent investigation per your request. Information for OCR can be found at the following website: https://www2.ed.gov/about/offices/list/ocr/index.html?presrc

Lastly, you have requested that your grade adjudication petition be moved forward to formally review the grade you received in the NS06 independent study course. Your petition will be reviewed and the grade adjudication process will be implemented as requested.

University promised to conduct the grade adjudication as the student requested on January 24, 2024

Regards,
Dr. Adair

Request made on January 24, 2024

From: Oliver, Germine <gbanS027@psu.edu>
Sent: Wednesday, January 24, 2024 3:28 PM
To: Hupsog, Judith F <jhupsog@psu.edu>; Badusk, Laurie <ltb340@psu.edu>; Matter, Sheri <sxm169@psu.edu>; Wright Watson, Denita Renee <Denita@psu.edu>; Adair, Suzanne <sla917@psu.edu>; Fong, Duncan King-Hoi <z7x@psu.edu>; Grad Dean's Office <gradeansoffice@psu.edu>; Oman, Tabitha <txt1152@psu.edu>
Subject: Grade Adjudication request

DUE PROCESS VIOLATIONS EVIDENCE

Hello,

To whom it may concern,

Below is my formal request for a grade adjudication in the NS06 independent study (Fall 2023).

The grade received violates school policy 47-20. The instructor did not provide a written (paper or electronic form) notification of the basis for grades to me on or before the first class meeting.

Also, I have been informed in an email correspondence by a representative from the office of Affirmative Action that I am being terminated from the nursing program for missing previously specified deadlines. This is another excuse to justify a blatant discriminatory act against my person at Penn State University. I intend to challenge these unsubstantiated claims as vigorously as Penn State policy guidelines would allow. It is my understanding that there are no such stipulation neither in school policy nor in the student handbook for the DNP program. I completed all the benchmarks and other requirements, as specified in the DNP program and within the prescribed timeline, except for the oral presentation, which is beyond my purview.

I intend to appeal any arbitrary decisions if and when they are communicated to me officially.

Please see attached document for the grade adjudication.

Germine Oliver

From: Matter, Sheri <sxm189@psu.edu>
Sent: Wednesday, February 7, 2024 9:23 AM
To: Oliver, Germine A <gobien507@psu.edu>; BOBADILA@CENTURYLINK.NET <BOBADILA@CENTURYLINK.NET>
Cc: Matter, Sheri <sxm189@psu.edu>
Subject: Email Access and Grade Adjudication

University responded to the January 24, 2024 request on February 7, 2024 and placed the dismissal on "hold"

Good Afternoon Germine:

Per your request, the grade adjudication process will be implemented. According to University policy G-10, the process begins with the following steps:

1. A student who wishes to question or challenge the grade must first discuss grading practices and assignments with the instructor. It is expected that the student and instructor will try to eliminate any misunderstandings and will attempt to work out any disagreements over grades.

2. On the rare occasion that a student and instructor fail to resolve the grade dispute through informal means, the student should request grade mediation from the head of the academic program offering the course who will review the issue and take appropriate action to seek resolution.

Therefore, if you haven't already done so, your first task is to contact Dr. Kelly Wolgast to discuss the matter as stated above to see if the issue can be resolved. If there is no resolution, you will need to contact Dr. Sheri Matter, the DNP Program Head, to request a review of your grade.

2.8.2024, 11:40 PM

https://outlook.office.com/mail/messages/id/AAQkAGQ1AAn7LzfOg1...

If the grade dispute is not resolved through the first two steps above, then Associate Dean Judith Hupsog will review your formal petition and seek any additional information she may need from you, the instructor, or others to determine if there is evidence that the instructor's assignment of the grade is in violation of Senate Policy 47-20. The Program Head will let Dean Kodish know whether the issue has been resolved through either of the steps above or if the formal problem needs to move to the next step of being reviewed by her. While your grade is being reviewed your termination from the program has been placed on hold.

SON, WOLDEN OLIVER, TARGETED
BY THE US ARMY AND TORTURED
TO PROTECT PENN STATE JULY-
AUGUST 2025

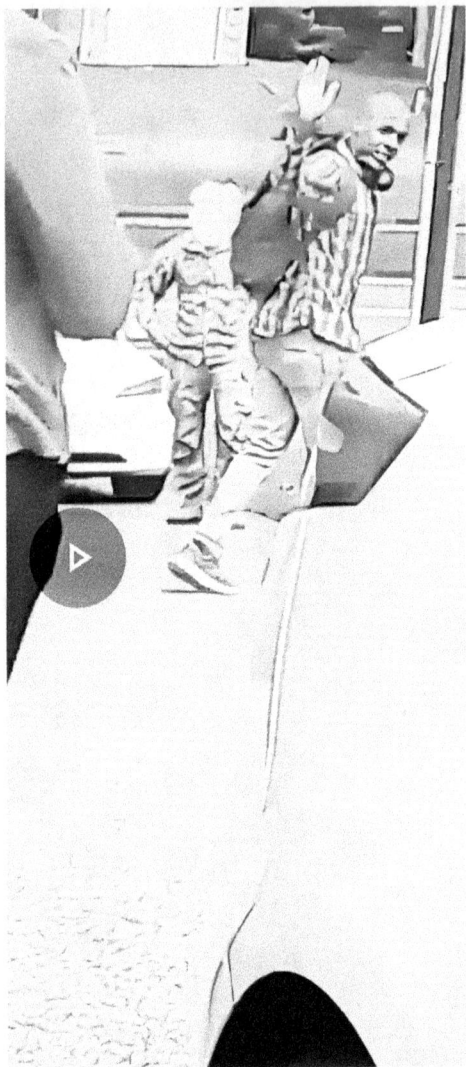

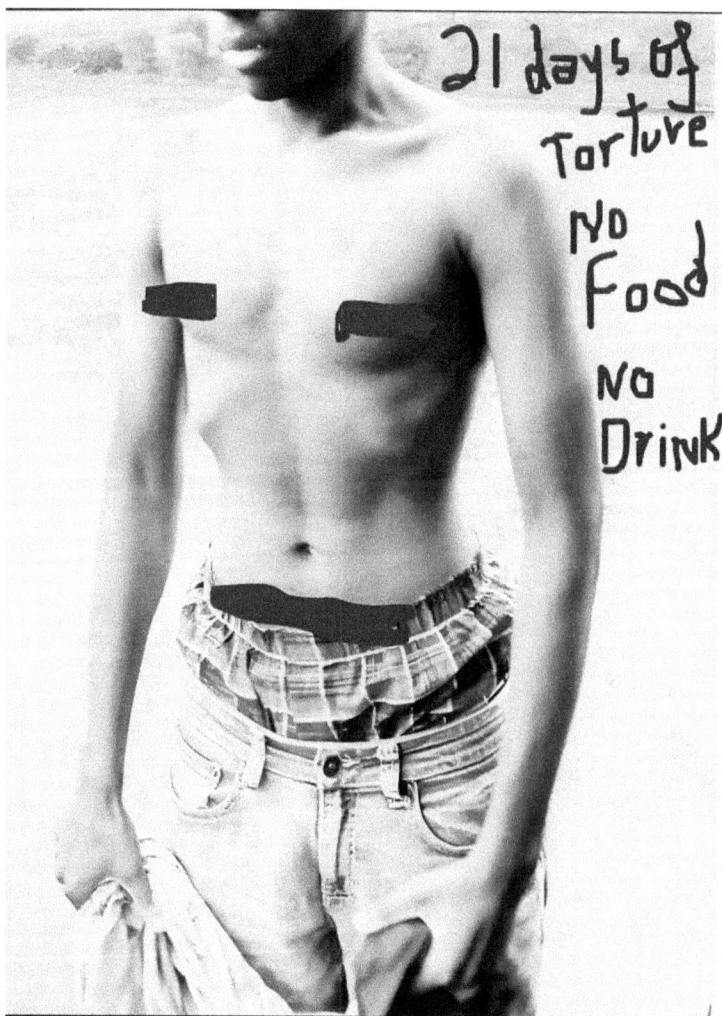

FAMILY IS TARGETED ON TWITTER
IN TWO OCCASIONS TO PROTECT
PENN STATE APRIL AND JULY 2025

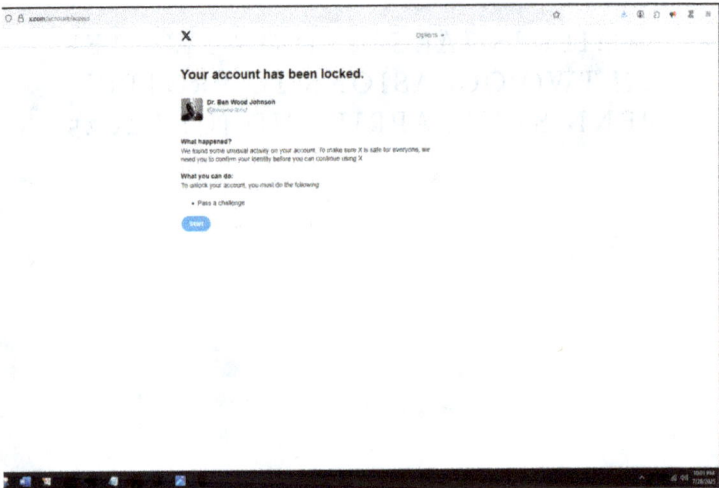

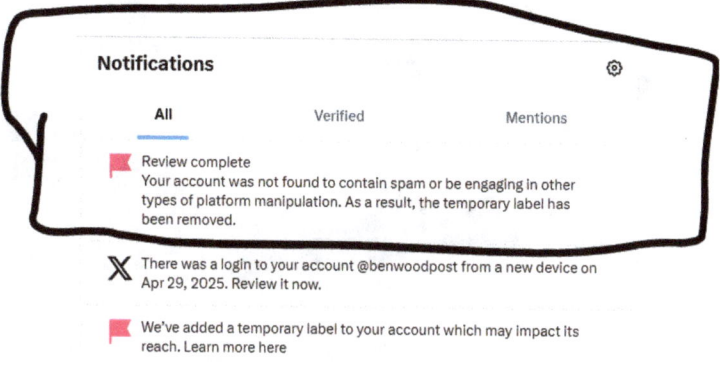

There was a login to your account @benwoodpost from a new device on Apr 29, 2025. Review it now.

We've added a temporary label to your account which may impact its reach. Learn more here

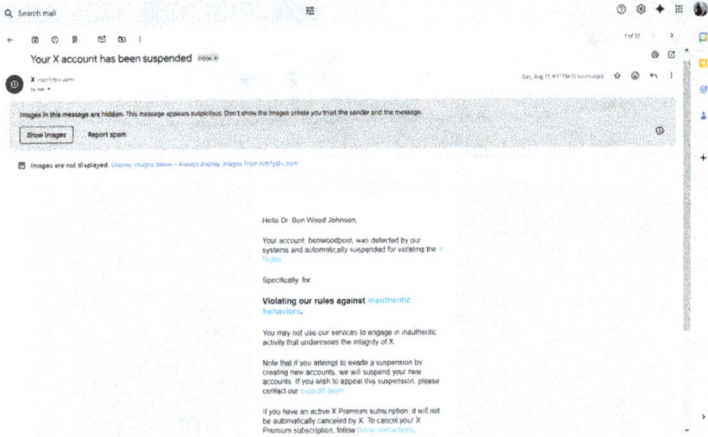

CRIMINAL CONSPIRACY AND
SILENCE AMONG STATE OFFICIALS
TO PROTECT PENN STATE

Network of Notice and Silence Surrounding PHRC Misconduct

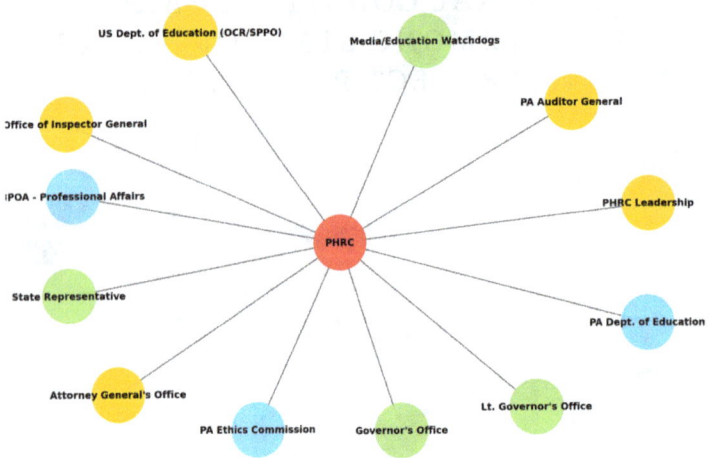

CONVERSATION WITH PENN STATE
BOARD OF TRUSTEES AND
UNIVERSITY PRESIDENT APRIL 2024

Mr. Johnson,

As Senior Vice President and Chief of Staff, I help President Bendapudi respond to emails and important issues. Thank you for your email. We have been informed that the Grade Adjudication process has been concluded with the Dean's review and decision, which is final. Additionally, we understand that the Office of Equal Opportunity and Access (formerly the Affirmative Action Office) has directed you to contact the Department of Education's Office of Civil Rights with any further concerns, and that you have filed a complaint with the Pennsylvania Department of Education, which the University will respond to as required. Based on this information, there will be no further action taken and the matter is considered closed.

Sincerely,

Michael Wade Smith
Senior Vice President and Chief of Staff

From: germine and benjamin <bobadilo@centurylink.net>
Sent: Monday, April 15, 2024 3:09 PM
To: Harvey, Shannon S <sxs205@psu.edu>; Office of the President <president@psu.edu>; Harlow, Bernadeen R <brh12@psu.edu>; bot@psu.edu; Redding, Russell Charles <rcr132@psu.edu>; Mumin, Khalid N <kxm340@psu.edu>; Dunn, Cynthia A <cad46@psu.edu>
Subject: Urgent Appeal for Immediate Intervention in Case of Discrimination and Fraudulent Conduct at Penn State University
Importance: High

> Some people who received this message don't often get email from bobadilo@centurylink.net. Learn why this is important

April 15, 2024
Dear Members of the Penn State Board of Trustees,
I am writing to you as a deeply concerned husband and father, seeking your immediate attention and intervention in a matter that has caused immense distress to my family. My wife, Germine Oliver, a student at Penn State University's Ross and Carol Nese College of Nursing, has been subjected to a pattern of discrimination, harassment, and retaliation by faculty members and university administrators. This unacceptable treatment has not only jeopardized her academic future but has also taken a severe toll on our entire family's well-being.
Despite our repeated efforts to resolve this issue through the proper channels, we have been met with resistance, disregard for due process, and a shocking lack of accountability from the university. Penn State has not only dismissed my wife without proper cause or procedure but has also refused to conduct an independent review of her case, despite numerous requests. Instead, they have resorted to making false statements and mischaracterizing her academic record to justify their actions.

The situation has escalated even further with the recent discovery of fraudulent conduct by the Dean of the College of Nursing, Laurie Badzek. In an official letter dated April 8, 2024, Dean Badzek made demonstrably false claims about my wife's academic progress, citing a non-existent course to uphold a failing grade and outside the scope of existing school policies. This blatant misrepresentation of her record is not only a breach of trust but also a clear violation of the principles of academic integrity and fairness that Penn State claims to uphold.

As a result of this ongoing mistreatment and the university's refusal to address our concerns, my wife's academic standing and future prospects have been severely compromised. Moreover, the emotional distress and mental anguish caused by this ordeal have taken an immense toll on our entire family. We are losing faith in the institution that is supposed to nurture and support its students, not harm and hinder them.

I implore you, as members of the Board of Trustees, to take immediate action to investigate this matter thoroughly and hold the responsible parties accountable for their actions. The fraudulent conduct and discriminatory treatment my wife has endured cannot be allowed to continue unchecked.

We need your leadership and intervention to ensure that justice is served and that no other student or family has to endure such mistreatment at the hands of Penn State University. As immigrants, we have no recourse in this country. Please, help us.

Our family is counting on you to uphold the values of integrity, fairness, and accountability that Penn State claims to embody. We urge you to act swiftly and decisively to address this grave injustice and restore our faith in the institution.

Thank you for your attention to this critical matter. We eagerly await your response and action.

Sincerely,
Benjamin W. Johnson
Husband of Germine Oliver

WEBMAIL.CENTURYLINK.NET - GERMINE AND BENJAMIN <BOBADILO@CENTURYLINK.NET>

RE: URGENT APPEAL FOR IMMEDIATE INTERVENTION IN CASE OF DISCRIMINATION AND
FRAUDULENT CONDUCT AT PENN STATE UNIVERSITY

> me
> president@psu.edu
> 4/22/2024 1:11 PM

From me ⩒
    bobadilo@centurylink.net
To president@psu.edu

Dear Mr. Smith,

Your email response on behalf of President Bendapudi is utterly unacceptable and represents a
complete dereliction of Penn State University's ethical responsibilities. Your dismissive tone and
refusal to even acknowledge, let alone investigate, the grave allegations of discrimination, harassment,
retaliation, and outright fraud committed by university officials against my wife is reprehensible.

The evidence provided of the Dean fabricating non-existent course codes and intentionally
misrepresenting my wife's academic record is grounds for immediate termination at any respectable
institution. Yet, you have chosen to simply ignore this egregious breach of integrity and due process.
Your indifference to credible evidence of unethical and potentially unlawful conduct by administrators
is enabling a toxic culture of unaccountability to fester at Penn State.

My family has been put through severe emotional trauma and had our faith in this university
completely shattered by the discriminatory treatment and fraudulent actions we have endured. Yet, your
email displays a startling lack of compassion and fundamental disregard for upholding the principles of
fairness and justice that Penn State claims to embody.

Make no mistake - I will not allow you or Penn State's leadership to sweep these very serious
allegations under the rug through callous inaction. Your attempt to simply declare this "matter closed"
without a full and impartial investigation is an insult to academic integrity.

I am also a victim in this affair. Penn State University terminated me after I complained about the
treatment university officials had been inflicting to my wife. Given that I have all the information
pertinent to this case, I intend to advocate tirelessly for my rights and my wife's rights through every
available channel until this grave injustice is properly addressed. As both an alumnus and a former
employee who has experienced firsthand the issues at stake, my commitment to seeking justice is not
only for my wife but also in upholding the integrity of an institution I once held in high regard. I have a
duty to hold the university and university officials accountable for their misconduct.

Consider this email a notice that I will exhaustively pursue legal recourse and engage all relevant
government authorities if Penn State continues to stonewall and protect those who have so blatantly
violated institutional policies and ethical standards. You have been given compelling evidence that
cannot be dismissed so easily.

I demand that you immediately initiate a truly independent investigation by outside parties into the discriminatory actions, fraudulent conduct, violations of due process and policies, and conspiracy to undermine my wife's academic standing. Those found culpable must face real consequences befitting such unacceptable behavior from an institution of higher learning. Anything less will be viewed as further enabling unethical governance.

Penn State's continued refusal to uphold its moral and likely legal obligations in this matter will be met with intense scrutiny and escalation through every available avenue. My family's faith and our future prospects should not be so carelessly cast aside to protect those guilty of violating the sacred trust placed in this university.

Yes, we are black immigrants. But that does not mean our rights do not matter or should not matter at Penn State. To suggest otherwise is the epitome of discrimination. Thus, our status as black immigrants does not diminish our rights. Any insinuation to the contrary not only compounds the discrimination but also blatantly disregards Penn State's commitment to diversity and inclusion.

For years, my family has been persecuted in Pennsylvania. I have been the target of discrimination and relentless assaults. The University that awarded me the highest academic degree has consistently belittled me and my family. Now, I have irrefutable evidence of that persecution.

Relying on your friends in high places or in the court system to side with you will not shield you forever, as history is watching.

La défaite du Droit est toujours provisoire! (The defeat of Law is always temporary!)

Sooner or later, Penn State University will have to answer to Pennsylvanians, the American people, or the world over for its egregious conduct against my family.

I urge you to re-evaluate your stance and commit to genuine accountability before this situation devolves even further.

Sincerely,
Benjamin W. Johnson

On Fri, 19 Apr, 2024 at 1:36 PM, Office of the President <President@psu.edu> wrote:

   To: germine and benjamin

CEASE AND DESIST THREAT FROM
THE PHRC JANUARY 2025

pennsylvania
HUMAN RELATIONS COMMISSION

Germine Oliver
667 Mount Gretna Road
Elizabethtown, Pennsylvania, 17022

Re: Germine Oliver v. Penn State; PHRC No. #202317185

January 9, 2025

Dear Ms. Oliver:

The Pennsylvania Human Relations Commission ("PHRC") is in receipt of correspondence regarding its November 6, 2024, decision to close your case in the above captioned matter. The PHRC is committed to its statutory duty to investigate complaints of discrimination and to enforce the Commonwealth's anti-discrimination laws. This commitment extends to ensuring that all citizens of the Commonwealth, who file discrimination claims with our office, receive a fair and impartial decision from the PHRC, free from any outside influence.

Discrimination is insidious and often difficult to prove.   While it is understandable that you are upset and disagree with the PHRC's decision, every decision is reached after a fair and impartial review of the evidence. All matters are handled in a manner consistent with professional ethics and decisions are made based on the application of the law.   The PHRC utilizes trained investigators to review the evidence. Following the completion of an investigation, Executive Director, Chad Lassiter, signs the closure letter.   Executive Director Lassiter's signature merely acknowledges that he approved the final outcome; however, he is not involved in the investigation.   As such, we refute any allegation that Executive Director Lassiter was in any way influenced by the Respondent in this matter.

As Executive Director of the PHRC, and as a well-regarded expert in the field of social justice, Executive Director Lassiter is often called upon to speak to communities, community leaders and various entities across the Commonwealth, including universities such as Penn State.   Executive Director Lassiter is prohibited from accepting a fee for any speaking engagements and was not paid a fee for his speech at the black history event held at Penn State.

We note that you have taken advantage of the legal recourse available to you and have filed a Request for Preliminary Hearing. As such, there will be an additional review of your claim by the Office of Chief Counsel. This additional review will also be fair and impartial. It may take up to sixty days for you to be advised of the decision reached.

In the meantime, this correspondence serves as a formal request for Mr. Johnson to refrain from forwarding any additional correspondence on your behalf. He is neither a party to this matter nor an attorney representing your interest. Moreover, we further demand that Mr. Johnson cease and desist from asserting false claims against Executive Director Lassiter which serve to disparage his character and harm his reputation. Mr. Johnson's allegations of impropriety are baseless and without merit. Any further efforts to defame his character may be actionable in law.

Thank you for your attention to this matter. If you have any questions, please contact me or the Office of Chief Counsel at ra-hrphrcchiefcsl@pa.gov .

Sincerely,

Sandra Crawford, Chief Counsel
Pennsylvania Human Relations Commission

cc: Chad Lassiter, MSW
Executive Director

POLICE INTIMIDATION IN MAY 7 2024 AND OTHER IMAGES

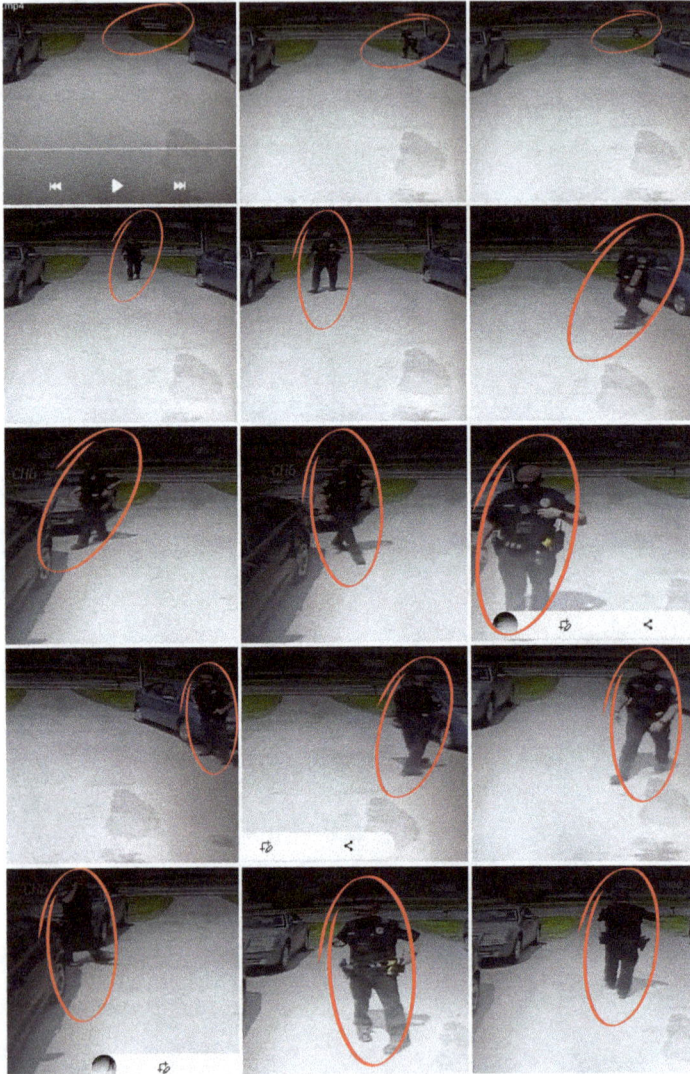

pennsylvania
HUMAN RELATIONS COMMISSION

EDUCATION INTAKE QUESTIONNAIRE

1. Complainant(s) Contact Information:

Name:	Wolden Oliver
Filing on behalf of:	Germine Oliver
Address:	▇▇▇▇▇▇▇▇
Address (Suite, Apt. etc.)	
City/State/Zip Code:	Elizabethtown, PA 17022
Email Address:	▇▇▇▇▇
Telephone No:	367-0102
Cell Phone No.:	
Date of Birth:	▇▇▇▇▇▇

Sex: Male   Race: Black   Are you Hispanic? ☐ Yes ☒ No

What is your National Origin?   United States of America

2. Respondent(s) Contact Information:

Name:	The Pennsylvania State University
Address:	201 Old Main
Address (Suite, Apt. etc.)	
City/State/Zip Code:	University Park, PA 16802
Telephone No:	865-7611

3. Protected Class(es) (check all reasons you have been discriminated against and specify the class, e.g., race, African American; sex, female):

☑	Race:	Black	☐	Ancestry:	
☑	Color:	Black	☐	Religious Creed:	
☑	Sex:	Female	☑	National Origin:	▇▇▇
☐	Disability:		☑	Retaliation:	for filing complaints
☐	Use of Guide or Support Animal:		☑	Other (specify)	Institutional Discrimination

4. The Pennsylvania county where you were harmed: Centre

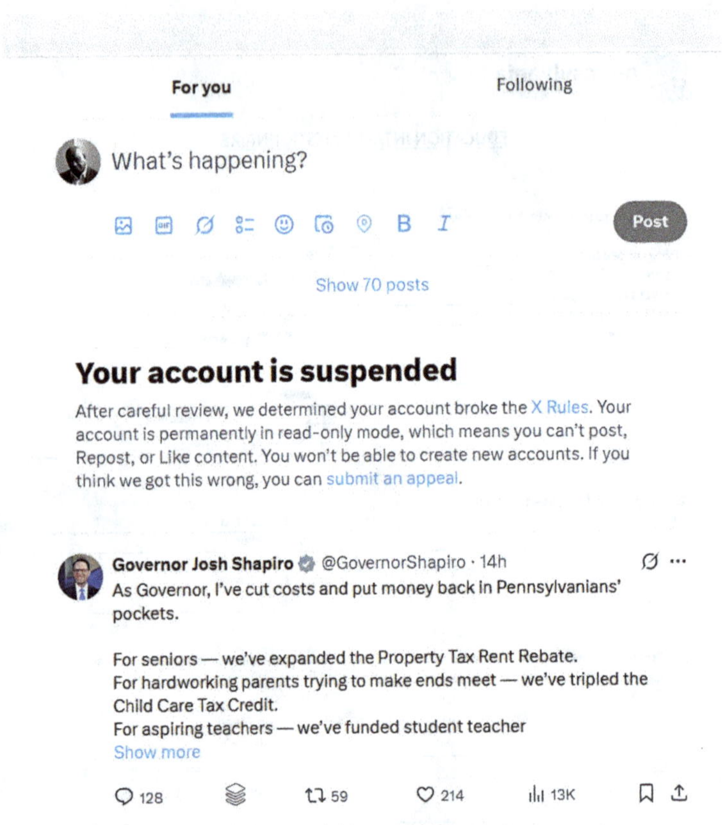
For you
Following
What's happening?
Post
Show 70 posts
Your account is suspended
After careful review, we determined your account broke the X Rules. Your account is permanently in read-only mode, which means you can't post, Repost, or Like content. You won't be able to create new accounts. If you think we got this wrong, you can submit an appeal.
Governor Josh Shapiro @GovernorShapiro · 14h
As Governor, I've cut costs and put money back in Pennsylvanians' pockets.
For seniors — we've expanded the Property Tax Rent Rebate.
For hardworking parents trying to make ends meet — we've tripled the Child Care Tax Credit.
For aspiring teachers — we've funded student teacher
Show more
128
59
214
13K

olay images from notify@x.com

Hello Dr. Ben Wood Johnson,

Your account, benwoodpost, was detected by our systems and automatically suspended for violating the X Rules.

Specifically, for:

Violating our rules against inauthentic behaviors.

You may not use our services to engage in inauthentic activity that undermines the integrity of X.

Note that if you attempt to evade a suspension by creating new accounts, we will suspend your new accounts. If you wish to appeal this suspension, please contact our support team.

If you have an active X Premium subscription, it will not be automatically canceled by X. To cancel your X Premium subscription, follow these instructions.

1 of 23   <   >

Sun, Aug 17, 9:17 PM (3 hours ago)   ☆   ☺   ↩   ⋮

♡ 9   ⬚   ⟲ 7   ♡ 20   ⬚ 1.2K   🔖 ⬆

Dr. Ben Wood Johnson ✔ @benwoodpost · 5m   [Promote] ⊘ ···
I WILL SELF-DEPORT IMMEDIATELY. I WILL LEAVE THIS LAND AS EARLY AS
TOMORROW IF THAT IS WHAT YOU WANT SO I DON'T HOLD YOU
ACCOUNTABLE FOR YOUR CRIMES AGAINST MY FAMILY. BUT PLEASE,
RELEASE MY CHILD. I SPENT MY LIFE PROTECTING MY WIFE AND
CHILDREN. YOU DESTROYED MY WIFE. NOW, YOU ARE DESTROYING MY
CHILDREN. RELEASE WOLDEN NOW. RELEASE MY CHILD NOW. YOU WILL
LEAVE ME NO CHOICE BUT TO REACT LIKE ANY FATHER WOULD. RELEASE
MY CHILD PEOPLE. RELEASE MY CHILD.

♡   ⬚   ⟲   ♡   ⬚ 4   🔖 ⬆

Dr. Ben Wood Johnson ✔ @benwoodpost · 11m   [Promote] ⊘ ···
IF THE GOAL WAS TO BREAK ME, I AM BROKEN. IF THE GOAL WAS TO
DESTROY ME, I AM DESTROYED. BUT RELEASE MY CHILD. RELEASE MY
CHILD. RELEASE MY CHILD.

♡   ⬚   ⟲   ♡   ⬚ 7   🔖 ⬆

Dr. Ben Wood Johnson ✔ @benwoodpost · 22m   [Promote] ⊘ ···
RELEASE MY CHILD NOW. FINAL WARNING!

♡   ⬚   ⟲   ♡   ⬚ 6   🔖 ⬆

Dr. Ben Wood Johnson ✔ @benwoodpost · Jul 26   [Promote] ⊘ ···
Please, do not humiliate my child any longer. Do not humiliate this family
any longer. Release my son immediately. Let him come home immediately,
as we requested. Leave us ALONE!

♡   ⬚   ⟲   ♡   ⬚ 9   🔖 ⬆

Who to follow

👤 Harmeet K. Dhillon and FBI Director Kash Patel follow

ENTCOM

ohne ✓
peaktruthtoyou

Follow

t Jackson
rtjackson

Follow

happening

Guardians at I
Starts at 11:10 AN

← **Fort Jackson**
@fortjackson ≫

RELEASE MY CHILD. Wolden Oliver committed no crimes. He should not be held anywhere against his will in these United States. I am about to break loose and I am warning you. I will allow you to humiliate my family any longer. RELEASE MY CHILD NOW. FINAL WARNING!

11:28 AM

ding

Jnited States
r

IF THE GOAL WAS TO BREAK ME, I AM BROKEN. IF THE GOAL WAS TO DESTROY ME, I AM DESTROYED. BUT RELEASE MY CHILD. RELEASE MY CHILD. RELEASE MY CHILD.

11:44 AM · Sent

retary

ce | Privacy Policy |

Start a new message ▷

ABOUT THE AUTHOR

BEN WOOD JOHNSON, PH.D.

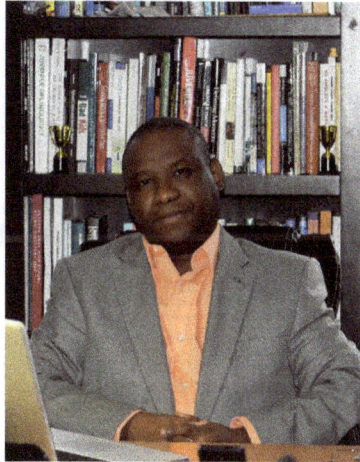

Dr. Johnson is a civil rights advocate, author, educator, and philosopher. He is a social observer. He is also a multidisciplinary researcher. He writes about philosophy, legal theory, public and foreign policy, education, politics, ethics, race, and crime.

Dr. Johnson holds a doctorate in educational leadership, a master's degree in political science, a master's degree in public administration, a master's degree in criminal justice, and a bachelor's degree in criminal justice. He has worked in law enforcement.

Born on April 12, 1975, in Port-au-Prince, Haiti, Dr. Johnson is native French speaker. He is also fluent in many languages, including, but not limited to, Creole, English, Spanish,

Portuguese, and Italian. Dr. Johnson enjoys reading, poetry, painting, and music.

ALSO BY BEN WOOD JOHNSON

Other relevant works by Dr. Johnson

Racism: What is it?

Sartrean Ethics

Jean-Paul Sartre and Morality

Forced Out of Vietnam

Natural Law

Cogito, Ergo Philosophus

International Law

Citizen Obedience

Jean-Jacques Rousseau

Pennsylvania Inspired Leadership

Adult Education in America

Striving to Survive

Postcolonial Africa